It's another great book from CGP...

This book is for anyone studying **Edexcel International GCSE Mathematics A** or the **Edexcel Level 1/Level 2 Certificate in Mathematics**.

It's packed with exam-style questions for every topic — and it's rounded off with two realistic practice papers to fully prepare you for your exams.

It even includes a **free** Online Edition you can read on your computer or tablet! (The Online Edition also includes printable answers to both the practice papers.)

How to get your free online extras

Just go to **cgpbooks.co.uk/extras** and enter this code...

2500 7314 7015 3979

By the way, this code only works for one person. If somebody else has used this book before you, they might have already claimed the online extras.

CGP — still the best! ☺

Our sole aim here at CGP is to produce the highest quality books — carefully written, immaculately presented and dangerously close to being funny.

Then we work our socks off to get them out to you — at the cheapest possible prices.

Contents

☑ Use the tick boxes to check off the topics you've completed.

Section Four — Geometry and Measures

Section Five — Pythagoras and Trigonometry

Section Six — Statistics and Probability

Practice Papers

How to get answers for the Practice Papers
Your free Online Edition of this book includes fully worked solutions
for Practice Papers 1 & 2 that you can print out. (Just flick back to
the first page to find out how to get hold of your Online Edition.)

Published by CGP

Editors:
Rob Harrison, Shaun Harrogate, David Ryan

Contributors:
Rosie Hanson, Alan Mason

With thanks to Jane Appleton and Ruth Wilbourne for the proofreading.

ISBN: 978 1 78294 218 4

Clipart from Corel®
Printed by Elanders Ltd, Newcastle upon Tyne

Based on the classic CGP style created by Richard Parsons.

How to Use This Book

- Hold the book <u>upright</u>, approximately <u>50 cm</u> from your face, ensuring that the text looks like <u>this</u>, not s̄ı̄ɥ̄ʇ̄. Alternatively, place the book on a <u>horizontal</u> surface (e.g. a table or desk) and sit adjacent to the book, at a distance which doesn't make the text too small to read.

- In case of emergency, press the two halves of the book together <u>firmly</u> in order to close.

- Before attempting to use this book, familiarise yourself with the following <u>safety information</u>:

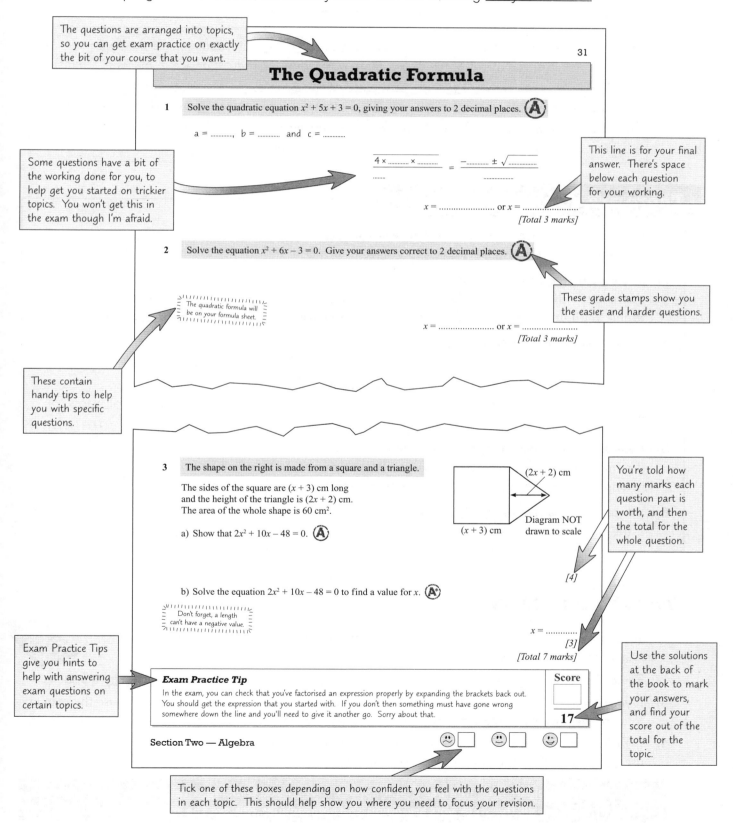

The questions are arranged into topics, so you can get exam practice on exactly the bit of your course that you want.

31

The Quadratic Formula

1   Solve the quadratic equation $x^2 + 5x + 3 = 0$, giving your answers to 2 decimal places. (A)

a = ..., b = ... and c = ...

$$4 \times \frac{\ldots \times \ldots}{\ldots} = \frac{-\ldots \pm \sqrt{\ldots}}{\ldots}$$

$x = ...$ or $x = ...$

[Total 3 marks]

Some questions have a bit of the working done for you, to help get you started on trickier topics. You won't get this in the exam though I'm afraid.

This line is for your final answer. There's space below each question for your working.

2   Solve the equation $x^2 + 6x - 3 = 0$. Give your answers correct to 2 decimal places. (A)

The quadratic formula will be on your formula sheet.

$x = ...$ or $x = ...$

[Total 3 marks]

These grade stamps show you the easier and harder questions.

These contain handy tips to help you with specific questions.

3   The shape on the right is made from a square and a triangle.

The sides of the square are $(x + 3)$ cm long and the height of the triangle is $(2x + 2)$ cm. The area of the whole shape is 60 cm².

a) Show that $2x^2 + 10x - 48 = 0$. (A)

$(2x + 2)$ cm

$(x + 3)$ cm

Diagram NOT drawn to scale

[4]

b) Solve the equation $2x^2 + 10x - 48 = 0$ to find a value for x. (A*)

Don't forget, a length can't have a negative value.

$x = ...$

[3]

[Total 7 marks]

You're told how many marks each question part is worth, and then the total for the whole question.

Exam Practice Tips give you hints to help with answering exam questions on certain topics.

Exam Practice Tip

In the exam, you can check that you've factorised an expression properly by expanding the brackets back out. You should get the expression that you started with. If you don't then something must have gone wrong somewhere down the line and you'll need to give it another go. Sorry about that.

Score

17

Use the solutions at the back of the book to mark your answers, and find your score out of the total for the topic.

Section Two — Algebra

Tick one of these boxes depending on how confident you feel with the questions in each topic. This should help show you where you need to focus your revision.

Exam Tips

Exam Stuff

1) If you're studying either the Edexcel Certificate or the International GCSE
   you will have <u>two</u> exams — you're allowed a calculator in <u>both</u> exams.

2) Both exams are 2 hours long and both are worth <u>100 marks</u>.

3) Timings in the exam are really important, so here's a quick guide...

> - As each paper is worth <u>100 marks</u> and you've got <u>120 minutes</u> to complete the paper,
>   you should spend about a <u>minute per mark</u> working on each question (i.e. 2 marks = 2 mins).
> - That'll leave you with <u>20 minutes</u> at the end of the exam to <u>check</u> back through your answers
>   and make sure you haven't made any silly mistakes. <u>Not</u> to just stare at that hottie in front.
> - If you're totally, hopelessly stuck on a question, just <u>leave it</u> and <u>move on</u> to the next one.
>   You can always <u>go back</u> to it at the end if you've got enough time.

There are a Few Golden Rules

1) **Always, always, always make sure you <u>read the question properly</u>.**
   For example, if the question asks you to give your answer in metres, <u>don't</u> give it in centimetres.

2) **Show <u>each step</u> in your <u>working</u>.**
   You're less likely to make a mistake if you write things out in stages. And even if your final answer's
   wrong, you'll probably pick up <u>some marks</u> if the examiner can see that your <u>method</u> is right.

3) **Check that your answer is <u>sensible</u>.**
   Worked out an angle of 450° or 0.045° in a triangle? You've probably gone wrong somewhere...

4) **Make sure you give your answer to the right <u>degree of accuracy</u>.**
   The question might ask you to round to a certain number of <u>significant figures</u> or <u>decimal places</u>.
   So make sure you do just that, otherwise you'll almost certainly lose marks.

5) **Look at the number of <u>marks</u> a question is worth.**
   If a question's worth 2 or more marks, you probably won't get them all for just
   writing down the final answer — you're going to have to <u>show your working</u>.

6) **Write your answers as <u>clearly</u> as you can.**
   If the examiner can't read your answer you won't get any marks, even if it's right.

> Obeying these Golden Rules will help you get as many marks as you can in the exam — but they're no use if you haven't learnt the stuff in the first place. So make sure you revise well and do <u>as many</u> practice questions as you can.

Using Your Calculator

1) Your calculator can make questions a lot easier for you but only if you <u>know how to use it</u>.
   Make sure you know what the different buttons do and how to use them.

2) Remember to check your calculator is in <u>degrees mode</u>. This is important for <u>trigonometry</u> questions.

3) If you're working out a <u>big calculation</u> on your calculator, it's best to do it in <u>stages</u> and use the <u>memory</u>
   to store the answers to the different parts. If you try and do it all in one go, it's too easy to mess it up.

4) If you're going to be a renegade and do a question all in one go on your calculator,
   use <u>brackets</u> so the calculator knows which bits to do first.

> REMEMBER: <u>Golden Rule number 2</u> still applies, even if you're using a calculator — you should
> still write down <u>all</u> the steps you are doing so the examiner can see the method you're using.

Prime Factors

1 Express 90 as a product of its prime factors.

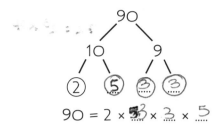

$$90 = 2 \times 3 \times 3 \times 5$$

....

[Total 3 marks]

2 Express:

a) 210 as a product of its prime factors.

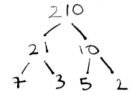

$$210 = 2 \times 3 \times 5 \times 7$$

[3]

b) 105^2 as a product of its prime factors.

....

[3]

[Total 6 marks]

3 Given that $25x^2 - 1$ factorises to give $(5x - 1)(5x + 1)$, express 2499 as a product of its prime factors.

....

[Total 3 marks]

Score: ☐

12

Common Multiples and Common Factors

1 Find:

   a) 72 as a product of its prime factors.

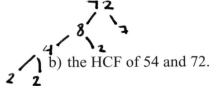

$72 = 2^3 \times 7$
....

[2]

   b) the HCF of 54 and 72.

....
[1]

   c) the LCM of 54 and 72.

....
[1]

[Total 4 marks]

2 Given that $A = 2^4 \times 3 \times 5^3$ and $B = 3^4 \times 5^2 \times 7^2$, find the HCF of A and B.

....
[Total 2 marks]

3 Find the LCM of 6, 8 and 10.

....
[Total 2 marks]

4 Two remote-control cars start at the same time from the start line on a track.

One car takes half a minute to complete a circuit.
The other car takes 1 minute 10 seconds to complete a circuit.

If they start side by side, how long will it be before they are next side by side
on the start line? State the units in your answer.

....
[Total 2 marks]

Score:

10

Fractions

1   Show that:

a) $\dfrac{4}{12} + \dfrac{3}{5} = \dfrac{14}{15}$

[2]

b) $\dfrac{9}{10} - \dfrac{2}{8} = \dfrac{13}{20}$

[2]
[Total 4 marks]

2   Work out:

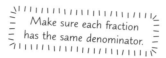
Make sure each fraction has the same denominator.

a) $3\dfrac{1}{2} + 2\dfrac{3}{5}$

....
[3]

b) $3\dfrac{3}{4} - 2\dfrac{1}{3}$

....
[3]
[Total 6 marks]

3   If $a = \dfrac{3}{4}$ and $b = 2\dfrac{1}{2}$, find the value of $\dfrac{1}{a} + \dfrac{1}{b}$.

....
[Total 3 marks]

4   Work out the following, giving your answers as fractions in their simplest form.

a) $1\dfrac{2}{3} \times \dfrac{9}{10}$

....
[3]

b) $3\dfrac{1}{7} \times 1\dfrac{1}{7}$

....
[2]
[Total 5 marks]

5 Give your answers to the following in their simplest form.

a) $\frac{3}{8} \div \frac{9}{10}$

....
[2]

b) $3\frac{1}{2} \div 1\frac{3}{4}$

....
[3]

[Total 5 marks]

6 Lisa is rearranging the dresses in her wardrobe.

$\frac{1}{3}$ of her dresses are black.

$\frac{1}{6}$ of her dresses are red.

$\frac{1}{4}$ of her dresses are blue.

a) What fraction of her dresses are not black, red or blue?
Give your answer in its simplest form.

....
[3]

b) Half of Lisa's blue dresses have sleeves.

Work out the smallest possible number of dresses Lisa could have in her wardrobe.

....
[3]

[Total 6 marks]

Score:

29

Fractions and Recurring Decimals

1 Write $\frac{10}{11}$ as a recurring decimal.

....
[Total 1 mark]

2 Write $\frac{7}{33}$ as a recurring decimal.

....
[Total 1 mark]

3 Write each of the following in the form $\frac{a}{b}$. Simplify your answers as far as possible.

a) $0.\dot{7}$ Let r = $0.\dot{7}$ *Start by naming the decimal.*

   so, 10r = ...

   10r − r = ... − $0.\dot{7}$

   9r = ...

   r = ...

....
[2]

b) $0.\dot{2}\dot{6}$

....
[2]

c) $1.\dot{3}\dot{6}$

....
[2]
[Total 6 marks]

4 Show that $0.5\dot{9}\dot{0} = \frac{13}{22}$

Hint: start by trying to get only the non-repeating part before the decimal point.

....
[Total 2 marks]

Score: ☐

10

 ☐   ☐   ☐

Section One — Numbers

8

Percentages

1   Ali has 40 micro pigs. 24 of them are female. (D)

What percentage of Ali's micro pigs are male?

.... %
[Total 3 marks]

2   Ben wants to buy a new laptop. His local shop sells two different laptops.
VAT is added at a cost of 20% of the laptop's original price.

a) Laptop A costs £395 before VAT is added. What is the total price including VAT? (D)

£ ....
[3]

b) The VAT on laptop B is £99. What is the total price of the laptop including VAT? (C)

£ ....
[3]

[Total 6 marks]

3   After an 8% pay rise Mr Brown's salary was £15 714. (C)

What was his salary before the increase?

£ ....
[Total 3 marks]

4   Last year Amy weighed 30 kg.

     a) Amy weighs 36 kg now. Calculate her percentage increase in weight.

                                                       .... %

                                                         [3]

     b) Amy is 12.5% taller than last year and she is now 135 cm tall.
        How tall was she last year?

                                                   .... cm

                                                         [3]

                                         [Total 6 marks]

5   Bill is looking at caravans.

     a) He sees one that cost £18 500 when it was new. It is now worth £12 600.
        Calculate the percentage decrease in value to 1 d.p.

                                                 .... %

                                                         [3]

     b) Another caravan has dropped 30% in value. It is now worth £11 549.
        What was its original value to the nearest pound?

                                       £ ....

                                                               [3]

                                         [Total 6 marks]

6   Between 1974 and 1994 the prize money for a football tournament increased by 25%.
     The prize money of the same tournament then increased by 16% between 1994 and 2014.
     By what percentage did the prize money increase between 1974 and 2014?

                                                   .... %

                                         [Total 3 marks]

Exam Practice Tip

One of the trickiest things about percentage change questions can be figuring out which type of question you're dealing with. Think carefully about whether the question is on percentage increase or decrease and whether you are being asked to find the amount after a % change, the actual % change or the amount before a % change.

Score

27

Section One — Numbers

Compound Interest and Depreciation

1   The population of fish in a lake is estimated to decrease by 8% every year.

Approximately how many fish will be left after 15 years if the initial population is 2000?

population after 15 years = $2000 \times \left(1 - \frac{\text{......}}{100}\right)^{\text{...}}$

$= 2000 \times (\text{............})^{\text{...}}$

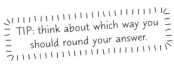
TIP: think about which way you should round your answer.

$= \text{...........................}$

.... fish

[Total 3 marks]

2   A new house cost £120 000, but increased in value by 15% each year.

Work out its value after 5 years, to the nearest £1000.

£ ....

[Total 3 marks]

3   A car dealership is selling a used car for £3995.
The car is 6 years old and its value has decreased by 11% each year.

Work out its original value to the nearest £100.

£ ....

[Total 3 marks]

4   Mrs Khan puts £2500 into a high interest savings account.
Interest is added to the account at the end of each year.
After 2 years Mrs Khan's account contains £2704.

What is the interest rate on Mrs Khan's account?

.... %

[Total 3 marks]

Score:

12

Ratios and Proportion

1 Eve is making a bird house. To make the walls, she takes a piece of wood that is 96 cm long and cuts it into four pieces in the ratio $5:6:6:7$.

How long is the longest piece of wood?

.... cm
[Total 3 marks]

2 Hannah is making some orange paint to paint the outside of her house.
She makes it by mixing together 15 tins of yellow paint and 6 tins of red paint.
The tins are all the same size.

a) Express the ratio of yellow to red paint in its simplest form.

....
[1]

b) Hannah used 1355 ml of yellow paint. How much red paint did she use?

.... ml
[2]
[Total 3 marks]

3 The vehicles at a motorshow are cars, motorbikes and hovercrafts in the ratio $13:5:1$.
If there are 286 cars at the show, what is the total number of motorbikes and hovercrafts?

....
[Total 3 marks]

4 Laura and Ashim are building scale models of a bridge.
Laura uses a scale of $1:38$ and her model is 133 cm long.
Ashim's model is 53.2 cm long.

What scale is Ashim using? Give your answer in the form $1:n$.

....
[Total 2 marks]

12

5 Last month a museum received £21 000 in donations.
They spent two thirds of the money on heating and lighting.
The rest of the money was spent on staff training and new exhibits in the ratio 2 : 5

How much did they spend on new exhibits?

£ ....
[Total 3 marks]

6 Ishmael has bought 23 identical glass slippers for £86.25.

Work out the total cost of 35 of these slippers.

£ ....
[Total 2 marks]

7 Here is a list of ingredients for making flapjacks.

Simple Flapjack Recipe
(Makes 12)

250 g oats   150 g butter
75 g sugar   75 g syrup

a) Elenni is making 18 flapjacks. How much butter does she need?

.... g
[2]

b) Jo has 300 g of syrup. What is the maximum number of flapjacks she can make?

....
[2]

[Total 4 marks]

Score:

20

Rounding Numbers and Estimating

1   Use your calculator to work out $\dfrac{197.8}{\sqrt{0.01+0.23}}$ Ⓒ

a) Write down all the figures on your calculator display.

....

[2]

b) Write down your answer to part a) correct to 3 significant figures.

....

[1]

[Total 3 marks]

2   Use your calculator to work out $\sqrt{\dfrac{12.71+137.936}{\cos 50° \times 13.2^2}}$ Ⓒ

a) Write down all the figures on your calculator display.

....

[2]

b) Write down your answer to part a) correct to 2 decimal places.

....

[1]

[Total 3 marks]

3   Look at the following calculation: $\dfrac{215.7 \times 44.8}{460}$ Ⓒ

a) By rounding each of the numbers to 1 significant figure, give an estimate for $\dfrac{215.7 \times 44.8}{460}$.

....

[3]

b) Without using your calculator, will your answer to part a) be larger or smaller than the exact answer? Explain why.

....

....

[2]

[Total 5 marks]

Score: ☐

11

Section One — Numbers

Bounds

1 Harry measures the height of his desk to be 62 cm when rounded to 2 s.f. **C**

a) Write down the upper bound of the measurement.

.... cm
[1]

b) Write down the lower bound of the measurement.

.... cm
[1]

[Total 2 marks]

2 Given that $x = 2.2$ correct to 1 decimal place,
write down the upper and lower bounds of $4x + 3$. **A**

Upper bound: ....

Lower bound: ....

[Total 4 marks]

3 The width of a rectangular piece of paper is 23.6 centimetres, correct to 1 decimal place. **A**
The length of the paper is 54.1 centimetres, correct to 1 decimal place.

a) Write down the lower bound for the length of the paper.

.... cm
[1]

b) Calculate the lower bound for the perimeter of the piece of paper.

.... cm
[2]

[Total 3 marks]

4 Here is a rectangle.
$x = 55$ mm to the nearest 5 mm. **A**
$y = 30$ mm to the nearest 5 mm.

Not to scale

Calculate the upper bound for the area of this rectangle.
Give your answer to 3 significant figures.

.... mm^2
[Total 3 marks]

5 Samantha is comparing the volume of two buckets. She measures the volume of each bucket to the nearest 0.1 litres and finds that bucket A has a volume of 8.3 litres and bucket B has a volume of 13.7 litres.

Calculate the lower bound of the difference, in litres, between the volumes of bucket A and bucket B

.... litres

[Total 2 marks]

6 Rounded to 1 decimal place, a triangle has a height of 3.2 cm and an area of 5.2 cm². Calculate the upper bound for the base length of the triangle, giving your answer to 2 d.p.

.... cm

[Total 3 marks]

7 Dan runs 100 m, measured to the nearest metre. His time is 12.5 s to the nearest tenth of a second.

Use the formula below to find Dan's speed to a suitable number of significant figures. Give a reason for your final answer.

$$\text{speed (m/s)} = \frac{\text{distance (m)}}{\text{time (s)}}$$

lower bound for distance = ... m   upper bound for distance = ... m

upper bound for time = ... s   lower bound for time = ... s

lower bound for speed = $\dfrac{............ \text{ m}}{............ \text{ s}}$ = ... m/s   upper bound for speed = $\dfrac{............ \text{ m}}{............ \text{ s}}$ = ... m/s

to 2 s.f. = ... m/s   to 1 s.f. = ... m/s   to 2 s.f. = ... m/s   to 1 s.f. = ... m/s

TIP: compare your upper and lower bounds.

....

....

[Total 5 marks]

Exam Practice Tip

If you're stuck in the exam wondering which bounds to use in a calculation, think about what would happen if you used the upper or lower bound for each of the numbers in your calculation. And remember that dividing something by a <u>bigger</u> number gives you a <u>smaller</u> number — and vice versa.

Score

22

Section One — Numbers

Standard Form

1 $A = 4.834 \times 10^9$, $B = 2.7 \times 10^5$, $C = 5.81 \times 10^{-3}$ Ⓑ

a) Express A as an ordinary number.

4834000000

[1]

b) Express C as an ordinary number.

0.581

[1]

c) Put A, B and C in order from smallest to largest.

C , B , A

[1]

[Total 3 marks]

2   The distance from Neptune to the Sun is approximately 4.5×10^9 km. Ⓑ
The distance from the Earth to the Sun is approximately 1.5×10^8 km.

Calculate the ratio of the Earth-Sun distance to the Neptune-Sun distance.
Give your answer in the form $1 : n$.

....

[Total 2 marks]

3   A cruise ship weighs approximately 7.59×10^7 kg. Ⓑ
Its passengers weigh a total of 2.1×10^5 kg.

a) Without using a calculator, find the total weight of the
ship and passengers. Give your answer in standard form.

You need matching powers to be able to add together two numbers in standard form.

.... kg

[2]

b) Express the weight of the passengers as a percentage of the total combined
weight of the ship and passengers. Give your answer to 2 decimal places.

.... %

[2]

[Total 4 marks]

Score: ☐

9

Section One — Numbers

Sets

1 $\xi = \{3, 5, 6, 8, 9, 11, 12, 14, 15\}$
   $A = \{\text{Even numbers}\}$
   $B = \{\text{Multiples of 3}\}$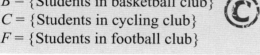

Write down the members of the following sets:

a) $A \cup B$

....

[1]

b) $A \cap B$

....

[1]

[Total 2 marks]

2 $\xi = \{\text{Students at Hilltop College}\}$
   $B = \{\text{Students in basketball club}\}$
   $C = \{\text{Students in cycling club}\}$
   $F = \{\text{Students in football club}\}$

Write a statement to interpret each of the following pieces of information.

a) $n(C \cap F) = 5$

....

[1]

b) $B \cap F = \varnothing$

....

[1]

[Total 2 marks]

3 $\xi = \{\text{Odd numbers}\}$
   $R = \{3, 5, 7, 9, 11, 13, 15\}$

Set S is a subset of R such that $R \cap S' = \{5, 7, 11, 13\}$ and $n(S) = 3$.
Write down the members of set S.

....

[Total 2 marks]

Score:

6

Section One — Numbers

Venn Diagrams

1   *L, M* and *N* are three sets. *L* and *M* are shown on the diagram below.

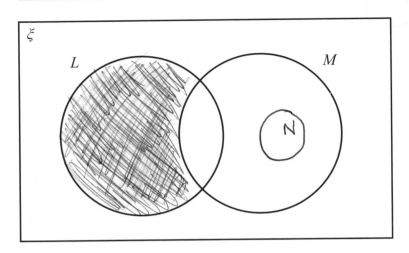

a) Shade the region represented by
$L \cap M'$

[1]

b) Given that $L \cap N = \emptyset$ and $N \subset M$,
draw the set *N* on the diagram.

[1]

[Total 2 marks]

2   *X* and *Y* are sets.

$n(\xi) = 40$
$n(Y) = 19$
$n(X \cup Y) = 31$
$X \cap Y = \{1, 2, 3, 4, 5, 6, 7, 8\}$

a) Complete the Venn diagram below to show the number of elements.

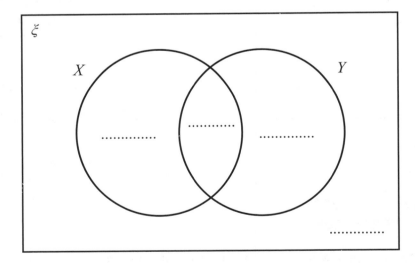

[2]

b) How many elements are in $X' \cap Y$?

....
[1]

c) Find $n(X' \cap Y')$.

....
[1]

[Total 4 marks]

Section One — Numbers

3 A cheese stall sells Cheddar, Wensleydale and Stilton. Sales are recorded over one week.

48 customers bought Cheddar. 28 customers bought Wensleydale. 52 customers bought Stilton.
10 customers bought both Cheddar and Wensleydale.
7 customers bought both Cheddar and Stilton.
No customers bought both Wensleydale and Stilton.

By drawing a Venn diagram or otherwise, find the number of customers the store had over one week.

....
[Total 3 marks]

4 The Venn diagram below shows the sets *A, B, C* and the universal set ξ.

Each number on the diagram represents the **number** of elements. Find:

a) n(*A* ∪ *C*)

....
[1]

b) n(*B* ∩ *C*′)

....
[1]

c) n(*A* ∩ *B* ∩ *C*)

....
[1]

d) n(*A*′ ∪ *B* ∪ *C*)

....
[1]
[Total 4 marks]

Score:

13

Section One — Numbers

Powers and Roots

1   Simplify the following.

a) $a \times a \times a \times a \times a \times a \times a$

a^7

[1]

b) $x^7 \div x$

x^6

[1]

c) $\dfrac{(d^9)^2}{d^4}$

d^{14}

[2]

[Total 4 marks]

2   Evaluate the following.

a) 3^0

1 ~~0~~

[1]

b) 5^{-2}

....

[1]

c) $8^{\frac{4}{3}}$

$$8^{\frac{4}{3}} = \left(8^{\frac{1}{3}}\right)^4 = (............)^4 = ...$$

....

[2]

[Total 4 marks]

3   Without using a calculator, write the following as single powers of 2.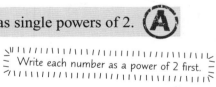

a) $2 \times 4 \times 8$

Write each number as a power of 2 first.

....

[2]

b) $\dfrac{(2 \times 2 \times 16)^2}{8}$

....

[3]

[Total 5 marks]

4 Simplify the following expressions fully.

a) $4a \times 6b$

....
[1]

b) $3a^3 \times 2ab^2$

....
[2]

c) $\dfrac{4a^5b^3}{2ab^2}$

....
[2]

[Total 5 marks]

5 Find the value of k in each of the following expressions.

a) $10^k = \dfrac{1}{100}$

$k = $ ....
[1]

b) $9^k = (\sqrt{9})^8$

$k = $ ....
[2]

c) $3^k = (3^4)^2 \times \dfrac{3^5}{3^{11}}$

$(3^4)^2 = 3^{\cdots \times \cdots} = 3^{\cdots} \qquad\qquad \dfrac{3^5}{3^{11}} = 3^{\cdots - \cdots} = 3^{\cdots}$

$(3^4)^2 \times \dfrac{3^5}{3^{11}} = 3^{\cdots} \times 3^{\cdots} = 3^{\cdots}$

$k = $ ....
[2]

[Total 5 marks]

6 Completely simplify the expression below.

$(9a^4)^{\frac{1}{2}} \times \dfrac{2ab^2}{6a^3b}$

....
[Total 3 marks]

Score:

26

Section Two — Algebra

Making Formulas from Words

1   A square has a side length of $3x$. **(D)**

a) Find a formula for the area, A, of the square in terms of x.

....

[1]

b) The value of x is 4 cm. What is the area of the square?

.... cm²

[1]

[Total 2 marks]

2   The total cost for a group of people having afternoon tea at a hotel can be worked out using the following rule. **(D)**

| Multiply the number of people by 10. | → | Add on the number of items of food that were eaten in total. | → | Total cost in pounds. |

a) Find a formula for the total cost of afternoon tea, C pounds, for p people eating a total of e items.

....

[2]

b) If 4 people went for afternoon tea and ate 8 items each, what would be the total cost?

£ ....

[2]

[Total 4 marks]

3   Peter and Marek are both travelling to London. **(C)**

Peter took the train. The train ticket for Peter's journey would normally cost £T, but Peter got it for half price because he had a railcard.

Marek took a taxi. The taxi fare costs £3 plus an extra 50p per mile.
Marek's journey was d miles long and he paid the same amount as Peter.

a) Show that $3 + 0.5d = \dfrac{T}{2}$.

[1]

b) The taxi journey was 2 miles long. How much would the train journey cost without a railcard?

£ ....

[2]

[Total 3 marks]

Score: ☐

9

Multiplying Out Brackets

1 Expand the brackets in the following expressions.
Simplify your answers as much as possible.

a) $3(x - 1)$

....
[1]

b) $4a(a + 2b)$

....
[1]

c) $8p^2(3 - 2p) - 2p(p - 3)$

....
[2]
[Total 4 marks]

2 Expand the brackets in the following expressions.
Simplify your answers as much as possible.

a) $(2t - 5)(3t + 4)$

....
[2]

b) $(x + 3)^2$

....
[2]
[Total 4 marks]

3 $a = 4(3b - 1) + 6(5 - 2b)$

Show that a is always equal to 26.

[Total 2 marks]

4 Write an expression for the area of the triangle below.
Simplify your expression as much as possible.

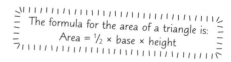
The formula for the area of a triangle is:
Area = ½ × base × height

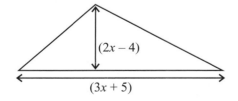
$(2x - 4)$
$(3x + 5)$

Diagram not accurately drawn

....
[Total 3 marks]

Exam Practice Tip

If you're struggling with double brackets in the exam, don't forget you can always use the <u>FOIL</u> method — multiply the <u>F</u>irst term in each bracket together, then multiply the <u>O</u>utside terms together, then the <u>I</u>nside terms, and finally multiply together the <u>L</u>ast term in each bracket... easy.

Score

13

Factorising

1   Factorise fully $4a^2 - 24ab$.

$$4a^2 - 24ab = 4(\text{.............} - \text{.............})$$
$$= 4\text{.......}(\text{.............} - \text{.............})$$

....

[Total 2 marks]

2   Factorise the following expressions fully.

a) $6x + 3$

....

[1]

b) $7y - 21y^2$

....

[2]

c) $2v^3w + 8v^2w^2$

....

[2]

[Total 5 marks]

3   Factorise the following expressions fully.

a) $x^2 - 16$

$$x^2 - 16 = x^2 - (\text{........})^2$$
$$= \text{...}$$

....

[2]

b) $9n^2 - 4m^2$

....

[2]

[Total 4 marks]

Score:

11

Manipulating Surds

1 Write $(2 + \sqrt{3})(5 - \sqrt{3})$ in the form $a + b\sqrt{3}$, where a and b are integers.

....

[Total 2 marks]

2 Find the value of a in the equation $\sqrt{45} + a\sqrt{5} = 10\sqrt{5}$.

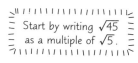
Start by writing $\sqrt{45}$ as a multiple of $\sqrt{5}$.

$a = $ ....

[Total 3 marks]

3 The expression $\dfrac{(\sqrt{27} + 6)}{\sqrt{3}}$ can be simplified to $a + b\sqrt{3}$, where a and b are integers.

Find the values of a and b.

$a = $ ....

$b = $ ....

[Total 3 marks]

4 $(\sqrt{3} + a\sqrt{5})^2 = b + 4\sqrt{15}$

Given that a and b are positive integers, find the values of a and b.

$a = $ ....

$b = $ ....

[Total 3 marks]

Score: ☐

11

Section Two — Algebra

Solving Equations

1   Solve the following equations.

a) $40 - 3x = 17x$ **D**

$x =$ ....
[2]

b) $2y - 5 = 3y - 12$ **D**

$y =$ ....
[3]

c) $2r - 6 = 3(3 - r)$ **C**

$r =$ ....
[3]

[Total 8 marks]

2   Solve the following equations.

a) $9b - 7 = 2(3b + 1)$

$b =$ ....
[3]

b) $\dfrac{28 - z}{4} = 5$

$z =$ ....
[2]

[Total 5 marks]

3   Solve this equation.

$\dfrac{8 - 2x}{3} + \dfrac{2x + 4}{9} = 12$

$x =$ ....
[Total 4 marks]

4 The quadrilateral below has a perimeter of 58 cm.

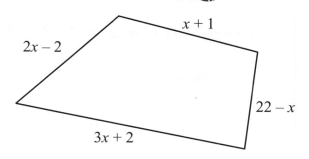

Diagram NOT
drawn to scale

All of the lengths on this diagram are in cm.

Find the value of x.

$x =$ ....

[Total 3 marks]

5 The diagram below shows two rectangles.
Rectangle A has sides of length $2x + 3$ cm and $5x - 8$ cm.
Rectangle B has sides of length $3x + 6$ cm and y cm.

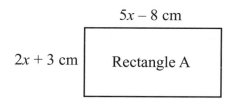

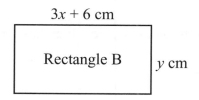

a) Rectangle B has the same perimeter as rectangle A.
   Write an equation for y in terms of x.

....

[3]

b) The perimeter of each rectangle is 32 cm. Find the value of y.

$y =$ ....

[3]

[Total 6 marks]

Exam Practice Tip

It's a good idea to check your solutions by substituting them back into the equation and checking that everything works out properly. It certainly beats sitting and twiddling your thumbs or counting sheep for the last few minutes of your exam.

Score

26

Section Two — Algebra

Formulas

1 The relationship between x and y is given by the formula $y = \dfrac{x-2}{3}$. **C**

   a) Rearrange this formula to make x the subject.

....

[2]

   b) Find the value of x when $y = 5$.

$x =$ ....

[2]

[Total 4 marks]

2 The formula for finding the volume of a pyramid is $V = \frac{1}{3}Ah$, where **C** A is the base area of the pyramid, and h is the height of the pyramid.

   a) Rearrange the formula to make h the subject.

....

[2]

   b) Find the height of a pyramid which has volume 18 cm³ and base area 12 cm².

.... cm

[2]

[Total 4 marks]

3 The formula $s = \frac{1}{2}gt^2$ is often used in physics. **B**

   a) Work out the value of s when $g = -9.8$ and $t = 8$.

$s =$ ....

[2]

   b) Rearrange the equation to make t the subject, where t is positive.

....

[2]

[Total 4 marks]

4 The relationship between a, b and y is given by the formula $a + y = \dfrac{b - y}{a}$.

a) Rearrange this formula to make y the subject.

....

[4]

b) Find the value of y when $a = 3$ and $b = 6$.

$y =$ ....

[2]

[Total 6 marks]

5 Rearrange the formula below to make n the subject.

$$x = \sqrt{\dfrac{(1 + n)}{(1 - n)}}$$

....

[Total 5 marks]

6 Make p the subject of $\dfrac{p}{5x} + \dfrac{px}{x + 4} = 2$ Ⓐ

Show your working and fully expand any brackets in your final answer.

TIP: try to get rid of
the fractions first.

....

[Total 5 marks]

Score:

28

Section Two — Algebra

Factorising Quadratics

1 Fully factorise the expressions below.

a) $x^2 + 4x - 32$

....

[2]

b) $3x^2 - 4x - 4$ (A)

....

[2]

[Total 4 marks]

2 The expression $5x^2 - 19x + 18$ is an example of a quadratic expression. (A)

a) Fully factorise the expression $5x^2 - 19x + 18$.

....

[2]

b) Use your answer to part a) to solve the equation $5x^2 - 19x + 18 = (x - 2)^2$.

....

[4]

[Total 6 marks]

3 The shape on the right is made from a square and a triangle.

The sides of the square are $(x + 3)$ cm long
and the height of the triangle is $(2x + 2)$ cm.
The area of the whole shape is 60 cm².

a) Show that $2x^2 + 10x - 48 = 0$. (A)

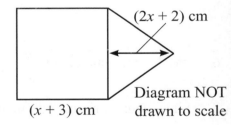

$(2x + 2)$ cm

Diagram NOT
drawn to scale

$(x + 3)$ cm

[4]

b) Solve the equation $2x^2 + 10x - 48 = 0$ to find a value for x. (A*)

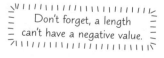
Don't forget, a length
can't have a negative value.

$x =$ ....

[3]

[Total 7 marks]

Exam Practice Tip

In the exam, you can check that you've factorised an expression properly by expanding the brackets back out.
You should get the expression that you started with. If you don't then something must have gone wrong
somewhere down the line and you'll need to give it another go. Sorry about that.

Score

17

The Quadratic Formula

1 Solve the quadratic equation $x^2 + 5x + 3 = 0$, giving your answers to 2 decimal places.

a = ...,   b = ... and   c = ...

$$x = \frac{-b \pm \sqrt{b^2 - 4ac}}{2a} = \frac{-............ \pm \sqrt{............^2 - 4 \times .... \times ....}}{2 \times ....} = \frac{-............ \pm \sqrt{............}}{............}$$

x = ... or x = ...

[Total 3 marks]

2 Solve the equation $x^2 + 6x - 3 = 0$. Give your answers correct to 2 decimal places.

The quadratic formula will be on your formula sheet.

x = ... or x = ...

[Total 3 marks]

3 Solve the equation $2x^2 - 7x + 2 = 0$. Give your answers correct to 2 decimal places.

x = ... or x = ...

[Total 3 marks]

4 Solve the equation $3x^2 - 2x - 4 = 0$. Give your answers in simplified surd form.

x = ... or x = ...

[Total 3 marks]

Exam Practice Tip

One thing you really need to watch out for when it comes to using the quadratic formula are those pesky minus signs. It's easy to get confused when you've got to subtract a negative number and you're under pressure in the exam. Just remember subtracting a negative number is the same as adding a positive number.

Score

12

Algebraic Fractions

1 Simplify the following algebraic fractions as much as possible.

a) $\dfrac{3x - 12}{x^2 - 16}$

....
[3]

b) $\dfrac{x^2 - 4}{x^2 + 8x + 12}$

....
[3]
[Total 6 marks]

2 Simplify the following.

a) $\dfrac{x^2}{3x} \times \dfrac{6}{x + 1}$

....
[2]

b) $\dfrac{10x}{3 + x} \div \dfrac{4}{5(3 + x)}$

....
[3]
[Total 5 marks]

3 Solve $\dfrac{3}{2x + 1} = \dfrac{7}{4x - 3}$. Show clear algebraic working.

....
[Total 4 marks]

4 Solve $\dfrac{12}{x + 4} + \dfrac{2}{x} = 3$, showing your working.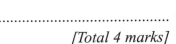

....
[Total 5 marks]

Score:

20

Inequalities

1 n is an integer. List all the possible values of n that satisfy the inequality $-3 \leq n < 2$.

....

[Total 2 marks]

2 Find the integer values of p which satisfy the inequality $9 < 2p \leq 18$.

....

[Total 3 marks]

3 Solve the following inequalities.

a) $4q - 5 < 23$

....

[2]

b) $\frac{2x}{5} \leq 3$

....

[2]

c) $x^2 + 1 > 37$

> Remember — when you take the
> square root you get two answers.

....

[2]

[Total 6 marks]

4 Possible values of x are given by the inequality $5 - 3x > 7 - x$.

a) Solve the inequality $5 - 3x > 7 - x$.

....

[2]

b) Represent your solution on the number line below.

[1]

[Total 3 marks]

Score: _____

14

Section Two — Algebra

Graphical Inequalities

1 Look at the grid below.

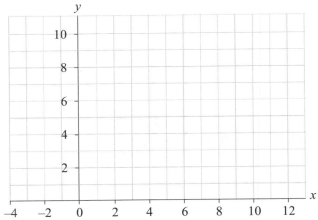

a) Use the grid to draw the graphs
    of $2x + y = 10$ and $y = x + 2$.

    [2]

b) Shade and label, using the letter S,
    the area represented by the inequalities
    $x \geq 1$, $2x + y \leq 10$, $y \geq x + 2$.

    [2]

    [Total 4 marks]

2 Look at the grid on the right.

On the grid, shade the region that
represents these inequalities:
$x < 5$
$y \geq -2$
$y - x \leq 1$

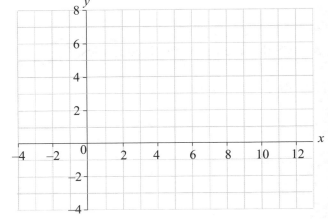

[Total 4 marks]

3 Look at the grid on the right.

The shaded region R is bounded by
the lines $y = 2$, $y = x$ and $x + y = 8$.

Write down three inequalities which
define R.

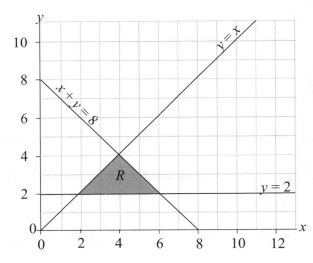

....

....

....

[Total 3 marks]

Exam Practice Tip

In the exam, you need to pay close attention to whether the symbol is just less than/greater than or whether it's
less than or equal to/greater than or equal to. If it's just less than/greater than you should draw a dashed line
to represent it on the graph. If it's less than or equal to/greater than or equal to you need to use a solid line.

Score

11

Section Two — Algebra

Simultaneous Equations and Graphs

1   The diagram below shows graphs of $2y - x = 5$ and $4y + 3x = 25$.

Use the diagram to solve these
simultaneous equations:

$2y - x = 5$
$4y + 3x = 25$

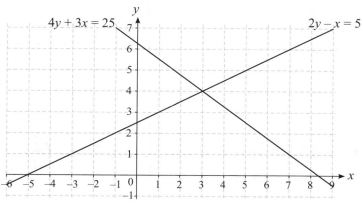

$x = $ .... $y = $ ....
[Total 1 mark]

2   The diagram below shows graphs of $y = x + 1$ and $y = 4 - 2x$.

a) Use the diagram to solve these
simultaneous equations:

$y = x + 1$
$y = 4 - 2x$

$x = $ .... $y = $ ....
[1]

b) By drawing another straight line,
solve these simultaneous equations:

$y = x + 1$
$3y = x + 9$

$x = $ .... $y = $ ....
[2]
[Total 3 marks]

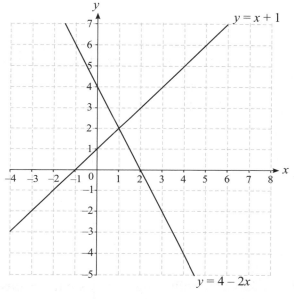

3   The diagram below shows part of the graph of $y = 4x - x^2$.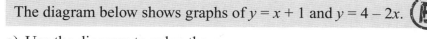

Use the graph to solve these
simultaneous equations.

$y = 5x - 2$
$y = 4x - x^2$

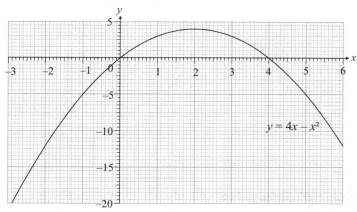

$x = $ .... , $y = $ ....

and $x = $ .... , $y = $ ....
[Total 3 marks]

Score: _____

7

Section Two — Algebra

Simultaneous Equations

1 Solve this pair of simultaneous equations.

$x + 3y = 11$
$3x + y = 9$

$x + 3y = 11 \xrightarrow{\times 3} 3x + \text{............} = \text{............}$
$\underline{3x + \quad y \;= \quad 9 \quad -}$

$\text{.........}y = \text{............}$

$y = \text{............}$

$x + (3 \times \text{............}) = 11$
$x = 11 - \text{............}$
$x = \text{............}$

$x = \text{............} \quad y = \text{............}$

[Total 3 marks]

2 Solve this pair of simultaneous equations.

$2x + 3y = 12$
$5x + 4y = 9$

$x = \text{............} \quad y = \text{............}$

[Total 4 marks]

3 Solve the following pair of simultaneous equations.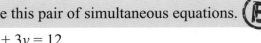

$x^2 + y = 4$
$y = 4x - 1$

$x = \text{............} \;, \quad y = \text{............}$

and $x = \text{............} \;, \quad y = \text{............}$

[Total 5 marks]

4 Solve the following pair of simultaneous equations.

$2x^2 + y^2 = 51$
$y = x + 6$

Substitution looks like the best way to go with this question.

$x = \text{............} \;, \quad y = \text{............}$

and $x = \text{............} \;, \quad y = \text{............}$

[Total 6 marks]

Exam Practice Tip

When you're solving simultaneous equations in the exam, it's always a good idea to check your answers at the end. Just substitute your values for x and y back into the original equations and see if they add up as they should. If they don't then you must have gone wrong somewhere, so go back and check your working.

Score

18

 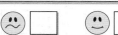

Direct and Inverse Proportion

1 The value of x is directly proportional to y^3. When $y = 3$, $x = 54$. Ⓐ

a) Write a formula for x in terms of y.

....
[3]

b) Calculate the value of x when $y = 4$.

$x = $ ....
[1]
[Total 4 marks]

2 c is inversely proportional to d^2. When $c = 2$, $d = 3$. Ⓐ

a) Write an expression for c in terms of d.

....
[3]

b) Find the values of d when $c = 0.5$.

....
[2]
[Total 5 marks]

3 A is directly proportional to the square root of T. When $T = 36$, $A = 4$. Ⓐ

a) Write an expression for A in terms of T.

....
[3]

b) Explain what happens to the value of A when the value of T halves.

[1]
[Total 4 marks]

4 The signal strength, S%, on Habib's mobile phone is inversely proportional to the distance, d km, he is from the nearest radio mast. Ⓐ

a) When Habib is 15 km from the nearest radio mast his signal strength is 60%.
Express S in terms of d.

....

[3]

b) On the axes to the right, sketch the graph of S against d.

[1]

[Total 4 marks]

5 If you hang an object on the end of a spring, the amount that the spring stretches by, x cm, is directly proportional to the mass of the object, M g. When $M = 40$, $x = 2$. Ⓐ

a) Write an equation connecting x and M.

....

[3]

b) How much would the spring stretch if an object with a mass of 55 g was hung on the end of it?

.... cm

[1]

[Total 4 marks]

6 Round a bend on a railway track the height difference (h mm) between the outer and inner rails must vary in direct proportion to the square of the maximum permitted speed (S km/h). When $S = 50$, $h = 35$. Ⓐ

a) Express h in terms of S.

....

[3]

b) Calculate h when $S = 40$.

....

[1]

[Total 4 marks]

Score: ☐

25

Straight Line Graphs

1 Draw the graph $2y + x = 7$ on the axes below, for values of x in the range $-2 \le x \le 10$.

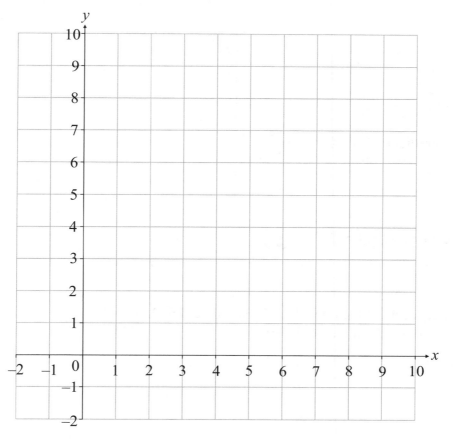

[Total 3 marks]

2 Point P has coordinates $(6, 2)$ and point Q has coordinates $(-4, 1)$.

a) Find the coordinates of the midpoint of PQ.

(................. , ...)
[2]

b) Point R has coordinates (a, b). The midpoint of PR is $(3, 5)$.
Find the values of a and b.

$a =$ ....

$b =$ ....
[3]

[Total 5 marks]

3 Line **L** passes through the points (0, –3) and (5, 7), as shown below.

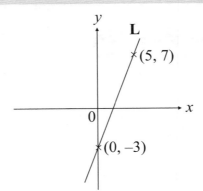

Diagram **NOT** to scale

a) Find the gradient of line **L**.

....

[2]

b) Find the equation of line **L**.

....

[1]

c) Find the equation of the line which is parallel to line **L** and passes through the point (2, 10).

....

[2]

[Total 5 marks]

4 The lines with equations $4y - 5x = 8$ and $3y - 2x = 20$ intersect at the point *M*.

a) Find the gradient of the line with equation $4y - 5x = 8$.

....

[3]

b) Find the coordinates of point *M*.

....

[5]

[Total 8 marks]

Score:

21

Section Three — Graphs, Functions and Calculus

Harder Graphs

1   This question is about the function $y = x^3 - 4x^2 + 4$.

a) Complete the table below.

x	-1	-0.5	0	0.5	1	1.5	2	2.5	3	3.5	4
y	-1	2.875	4	3.125	1	-1.625	-4				

[2]

b) Use your table to draw the graph of $y = x^3 - 4x^2 + 4$ on the grid,
for values of x in the range $-1 \le x \le 4$.

[2]

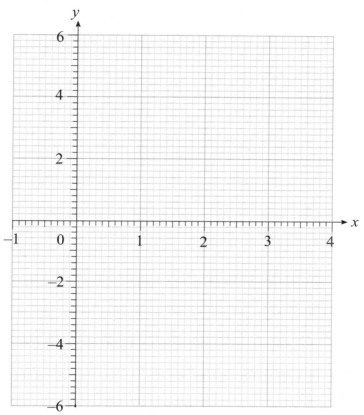

Don't use a ruler to
join up the dots in
curved graphs.

c) Estimate the solutions of the equation $x^3 - 4x^2 + 4 = 0$. Give your answers to 1 d.p.

....

[1]

d) By drawing a straight line on the grid, estimate the solutions to the equation $x^3 - 4x^2 + 2 = 0$.
Give your answers to 1 d.p.

....

[2]

[Total 7 marks]

2   This question is about the equation $y = x + \dfrac{4}{x} - 3$.

a) Complete this table of values.

x	0.2	0.5	1	2	3	4	5
y		5.5	2	1	1.333...	2	

[1]

b) On the grid below, draw the graph of $y = x + \dfrac{4}{x} - 3$ for $0.2 \le x \le 5$.

[2]

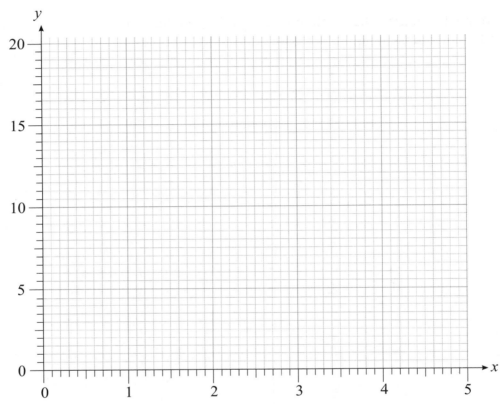

c) Use your graph to estimate the solutions of $x + \dfrac{4}{x} - 5.5 = 0$ in the interval $0.2 \le x \le 5$.
Give your answers to 1 d.p.

....

[2]

d) Draw a suitable straight line on your graph to estimate the solution to the equation $x + \dfrac{4}{x} - 3 = x$ in the interval $0.2 \le x \le 5$. Give your answer to 1 d.p.

....

[2]

[Total 7 marks]

Score

14

Section Three — Graphs, Functions and Calculus

Functions

1   f is a function such that $f(x) = \dfrac{3}{2x+5}$.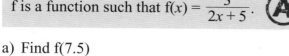

   a) Find f(7.5)

....

[1]

   b) State which value of x must be excluded from the domain of f(x).

....

[1]

   c) Find the inverse function f^{-1} in the form f$^{-1}(x)$. Show your working clearly.

f$^{-1}(x)$ = ...

[3]

[Total 5 marks]

2   f and g are functions such that $f(x) = 2x^2 + 3$ and $g(x) = \sqrt{2x - 6}$.

   a) Find g(21)

....

[1]

   b) Find gf(x)

     Remember to do the function closest to x first.

gf(x) = ...

[2]

   c) Solve fg(a) = 7

a = ...

[3]

[Total 6 marks]

Section Three — Graphs, Functions and Calculus

44

3 f is a function such that $f(x) = \sqrt{x^2 - 25}$.

a) Find $f(13)$.

....

[1]

b) Which values of x must be excluded from the domain of $f(x)$?

....

[2]

c) For what values of x does $f(x) = 1$?

....

[3]

The graph of $y = g(x)$ is drawn on the grid below.

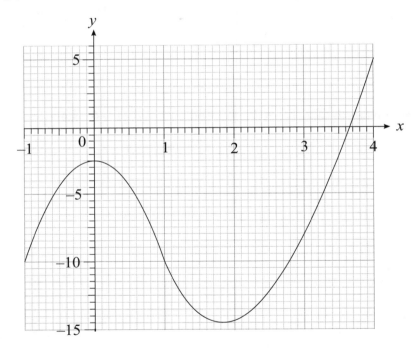

d) Find the exact value of $fg(1)$.

....

[2]

[Total 8 marks]

Score:

19

Differentiation

1 A curve has equation $y = 2x^3 + x^2 - 8x + 3$.

Find $\dfrac{dy}{dx}$.

$$\dfrac{dy}{dx} = \text{.................................}$$

[Total 2 marks]

2 A quadratic curve has the equation $y = -x^2 + 3$.

a) Find $\dfrac{dy}{dx}$. Ⓑ

$$\dfrac{dy}{dx} = \text{.................................}$$

[1]

b) Find the gradient of the graph of $y = -x^2 + 3$ at $x = -1$ and $x = 2$. Ⓐ

Gradient at $x = -1$: ....

Gradient at $x = 2$: ....

[2]

[Total 3 marks]

3 The curve with equation $y = 3x^2 + \dfrac{7}{2x}$ has one turning point in the region $x > 0$.

a) Find $\dfrac{dy}{dx}$. Ⓑ

$$\dfrac{dy}{dx} = \text{.................................}$$

[3]

b) Find the coordinates of the turning point of the curve with the equation $y = 3x^2 + \dfrac{7}{2x}$.
   Give your answers to 2 d.p.

(................. , ...)

[4]

[Total 7 marks]

Section Three — Graphs, Functions and Calculus

4 The height above ground level, h metres, of part of a roller coaster track can be modelled by the equation $h = -2x^2 + 15x + 12$ for $0 \leq x \leq 8$. (A*)

Find the maximum height of this part of the roller coaster. Show your working.

.... m

[Total 5 marks]

5 A rectangular airfield has a length of $5x + 1$ km and a width of $5 - 2x$ km, where $-0.2 < x < 2.5$.

a) Write an equation for the area, A km^2, of the airfield. Expand and simplify your final answer. (C)

....

[2]

b) Find $\frac{dA}{dx}$. (B)

....

[2]

c) Find the maximum area of the airfield. (A*)

.... km^2

[3]

[Total 7 marks]

6 The displacement, s metres, of an object from a fixed point after t seconds is given by $s = 2t^3 - 3t^2 + 8$ for $0 \leq t \leq 5$. (A*)

a) What is the velocity of the object after 4 seconds?

.... m/s

[3]

b) After how many seconds was the acceleration of the object zero?

.... seconds

[3]

[Total 6 marks]

Exam Practice Tip

Often in differentiation questions you'll just need to differentiate an equation, set it equal to 0 and solve. But sometimes you'll then have to substitute the value you found back into the original equation. So make sure you keep track of what you're working out and what the question is actually asking you for.

Score

30

Geometry

1 ABC is an isosceles triangle with AB = BC. ACD is a straight line.

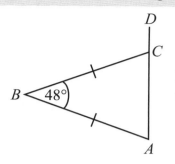

Diagram not accurately drawn

Work out the size of angle BCD.

.....................................°

[Total 3 marks]

2 BCDE is a trapezium with angle CDE = 90°. ABEF is a straight line.

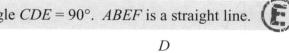

Diagram not accurately drawn

Work out the size of the angle marked x.

.....................................°

[Total 3 marks]

3 DEF and BEC are straight lines that cross at E.
AFB and AC are perpendicular to each other.

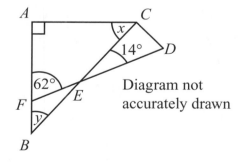

Diagram not accurately drawn

a) Find angle x.
Give a reason for each stage of your working.

Angles on a straight line add up to ....°,
so angle FEC = ...° − 14° = ...°

Angles in a quadrilateral add up to ....°,
so x = ...° − 90° − ....° − ....° = ...°

x = ...°

[2]

b) Use your answer to a) to show that y = 48°.

[2]

[Total 4 marks]

4 AB and CD are parallel lines. EF and GH are straight lines.

Work out the size of angle x.

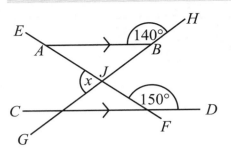

Diagram not accurately drawn

.... °

[Total 4 marks]

5 ABCD is a trapezium. Lines AB and DC are parallel to each other.

If you extend the lines in the diagram, it might be easier to see how to solve the problem.

Find the values of x and y.

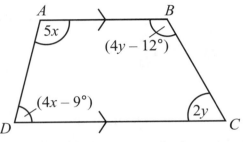

Diagram not accurately drawn

x = ... °   y = ... °

[Total 4 marks]

6 A, B and C are points on a circle, centre O. OA, OB and OC are radii of the circle.
OBD is a straight line and EF is the tangent to the circle at A.
Angle OCB = 27°, angle FDB = 142° and angle OAD is a right angle.

Find the size of angle AOC. Show your working clearly.

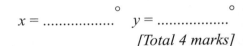

Diagram not accurately drawn

.... °

[Total 4 marks]

Exam Practice Tip

If you find yourself staring at a geometry problem in the exam not knowing where to start, just try finding any angles you can — don't worry tooooo much at first about the particular angle you've been asked to find.
Go through the rules of geometry one at a time, and apply each of them in as many ways as possible.

Score

22

Polygons

1 Part of a regular polygon is shown below. Each interior angle is 150°.

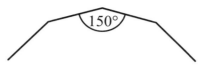

150°

Diagram not
accurately drawn

Calculate the number of sides of the polygon.

....

[Total 3 marks]

2 The diagram shows a regular pentagon and an equilateral triangle.

Work out the size of the angle *p*.

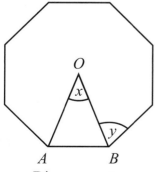

Diagram not
accurately drawn

°

....

[Total 3 marks]

3 The diagram shows a regular octagon. *AB* is a side of the octagon and *O* is its centre.

a) Work out the size of the angle marked *x*.

$x = $ .... °

[2]

b) Work out the size of the angle marked *y*.

$y = $ .... °

[2]

[Total 4 marks]

Section Four — Geometry and Measures

4   Six of the angles in the heptagon below are 140°, 137°, 128°, 109°, 152° and 134°.

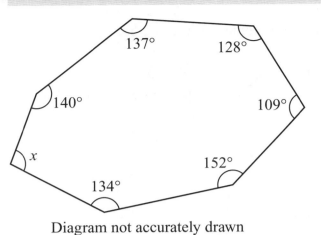

137°   128°

140°   109°

x   152°

134°

Diagram not accurately drawn

Find the size of angle x.

...........................°

[Total 4 marks]

5   *ABCDEF* is an irregular hexagon and *G* is a point on line *CD*.
   AB, *FG* and *ED* are parallel lines.

B   C
137°   y   G

117° D

A   x   151°

E

F
224°   Diagram not
accurately drawn

Find the size of angles *x* and *y*.

x = ...°   y = ...°

[Total 6 marks]

6   A regular polygon has 18 sides.

Prove that regular 18-sided polygons do not tessellate.

> A regular polygon tessellates if its interior angle divides into 360°.

[Total 3 marks]

Circle Geometry

1 The diagram shows a circle, centre *O*. *A*, *B*, *C* and *D* are points on the circumference.

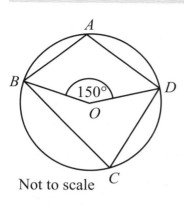

Not to scale

a) Work out the size of angle *BCD*. Give a reason for your answer.

....

....

[2]

b) Explain why angle *BAD* = 105°.

....

....

[1]

[Total 3 marks]

2 The diagram below shows a circle with centre *O*. *A*, *B*, *C* and *D* are points on the circumference of the circle and *AOC* is a straight line.

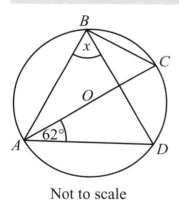

Not to scale

Work out the size of the angle marked *x*.

Angle *DBC* = ...°

Angle *ABC* = ...°

Angle *x* = ...° − ....° = ...°

x = ...°

[Total 3 marks]

3 Points *A*, *B* and *C* lie on the circumference of a circle and *DE* is the tangent to the circle at *A*. Angle *DAB* = 79° and angle *EAC* = 37°.

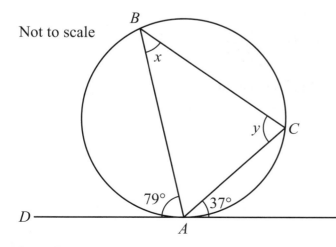

Find the sizes of angles *x* and *y*. Give a reason for your answers.

....

....

....

....

[Total 3 marks]

Section Four — Geometry and Measures

4 A, B, C and D are points on the circumference of a circle.
Angle BCD is 28° and angle ADC is 24°.

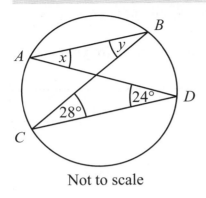

Not to scale

a) Find the sizes of angles x and y.

$x =$ ....° $y =$ ....°

[2]

b) Give a reason for your answers.

....

....

[1]

[Total 3 marks]

5   In the diagram, O is the centre of the circle. A, B, C and D are points on the
circumference of the circle and DE and BE are tangents. Angle DEB is 80°.

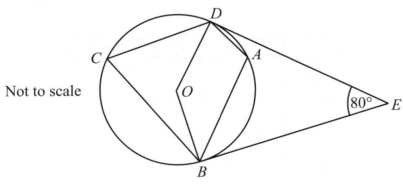

Not to scale

Work out the size of angle DAB.

..............................°

[Total 4 marks]

6   Points B, C, D and E lie on the circumference of a circle.
$AB = 6$ cm, $BC = 10$ cm, $AE = 8$ cm and $ED = x$.

Find the length of x.

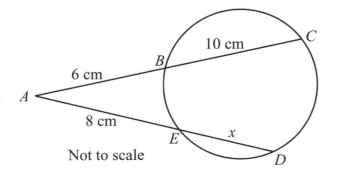

Not to scale

.... cm

[Total 2 marks]

Section Four — Geometry and Measures

7   Points *A*, *B*, *C*, *D* and *E* lie on the circumference of a circle with centre *O*.
AFD and CFE are chords of the circle. *AF* = 6 cm and *EF* = 9 cm.

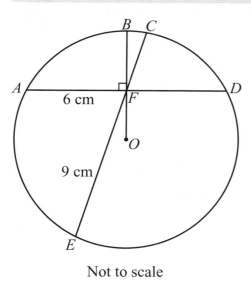

Find the length of *CF.*

Not to scale

.... cm

[Total 3 marks]

8   The diagram shows a circle with centre *O*. *A*, *B* and *C* are points on the circumference.
AD and CD are tangents to the circle and ABE is a straight line. Angle *CDO* is 24°.

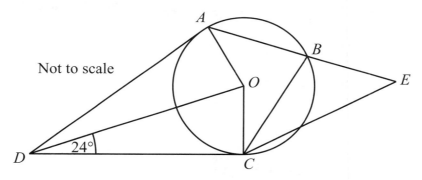

Find the size of angle *CBE*.

°

....

[Total 5 marks]

Exam Practice Tip

Make sure you know the rules about circles really, really well. Draw them out and stick them all over your
bedroom walls, your fridge, even your dog. Then in the exam, go through the rules one-by-one and use them to
fill in as many angles in the diagram as you can. Keep an eye out for sneaky isosceles triangles too.

Score

26

Section Four — Geometry and Measures

The Four Transformations

1 Triangle **A** has been drawn on the grid below. It has vertices at (2, 1), (5, 2) and (4, 4).

Reflect triangle **A** in the line $x = -1$. Label your image **B**.

Take each vertex of the triangle one-by-one, reflect them and then join them up.

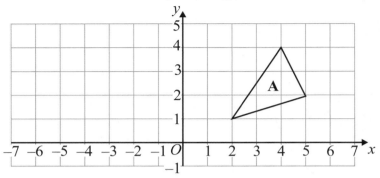

[Total 2 marks]

2 Shape **F** has been drawn on the grid below.

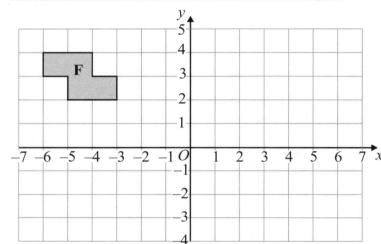

a) Translate shape **F** by the vector $\begin{pmatrix} 2 \\ -5 \end{pmatrix}$. Label your image **G**.

[1]

b) Rotate shape **F** by 90° clockwise around the point (0, −2). Label your image **H**.

[2]

[Total 3 marks]

3 In the diagram below, **B** is an image of **A**.

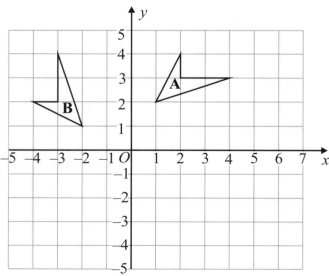

a) Describe fully the single transformation that maps **A** onto **B**.

....

....

....

[3]

b) Translate shape **B** by the vector $\begin{pmatrix} -1 \\ -4 \end{pmatrix}$. Label the image as **C**.

[1]

[Total 4 marks]

4 Shape **A** has been drawn on the grid below.

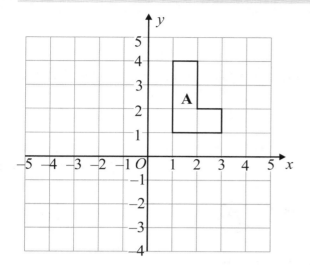

a) On the grid, reflect shape **A** in the *x*-axis. Label this image **B**.

[2]

b) Rotate shape **B** 90° clockwise about the origin. Label this image **C**.

[2]

c) Describe fully the single transformation which maps **A** onto **C**.

....

[2]

[Total 6 marks]

5 Triangle **R** has been drawn on the grid below.

Enlarge triangle **R** with centre (6, –3) and scale factor 4.
Label your image **S**.

[Total 3 marks]

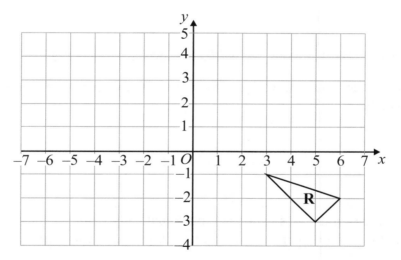

6 A triangle has been drawn on the grid below.

Enlarge the triangle by a scale factor of $\frac{1}{2}$ with centre of enlargement **C**.

[Total 3 marks]

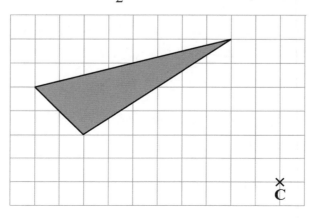

Score:

21

Section Four — Geometry and Measures

More Transformation Stuff

1 A parallelogram has an area of 7 cm².

The parallelogram is enlarged with scale factor 3. Work out the area of the enlarged parallelogram.

.... cm²

[Total 2 marks]

2 The diagram below shows two similar triangles, **A** and **B**.
The length of the base of each triangle is given.

Remember — two objects are similar if they're the same shape, but are different sizes.

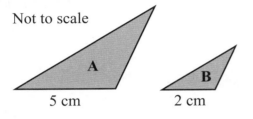

Not to scale

The area of triangle **B** is 6 cm².
Calculate the area of triangle **A**.

5 cm   2 cm

.... cm²

[Total 2 marks]

3 The radius of a tennis ball and the radius of a basketball are in the ratio 1 : 7.

Assuming both balls are spheres, work out the ratio of the volume of a tennis ball to the volume of a basketball.

....

[Total 1 mark]

4 **A**, **B** and **C** are three solid cones which are mathematically similar. The surface area of each cone is given below. The perpendicular height of **A** is 4 cm. The volume of **C** is 135π cm³.

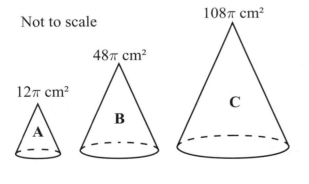

Not to scale

108π cm²

48π cm²

12π cm²

a) Calculate the volume of **A**.

.... cm³
[4]

b) Calculate the perpendicular height of **B**.

.... cm
[4]

[Total 8 marks]

Score:

13

Section Four — Geometry and Measures

Similarity

1   Triangles *ABC* and *DEF* are mathematically similar. Angles *BAC* and *EDF* are equal.

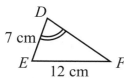

a) Work out the length of *AB*.

.... cm
[2]

b) Work out the length of *DF*.

.... cm
[1]

Not to scale

[Total 3 marks]

2   The shapes *ABCD* and *EFGH* are similar quadrilaterals.

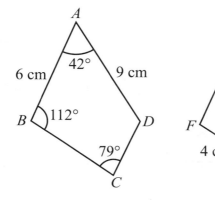

Not to scale

a) Find the length of *BC*.

.... cm
[2]

b) Find the length of *EF*.

.... cm
[1]

c) Find the size of angle *x*.

.... °
[1]

The area of quadrilateral *ABCD* is 36 cm².
d) What is the area of quadrilateral *EFGH*?

.... cm²
[2]

[Total 6 marks]

3 Two mathematically similar banners are shown below.

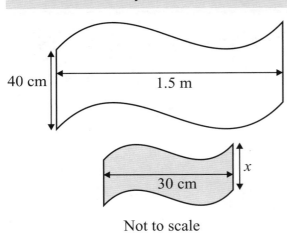

40 cm

1.5 m

30 cm

x

Not to scale

a) What is the length, in cm, of *x*?

.... cm

[2]

b) The area of the unshaded banner is 0.6 m².
What is the area of the shaded banner?

.... m²

[2]

[Total 4 marks]

4 *ABC* and *CDE* are similar triangles.

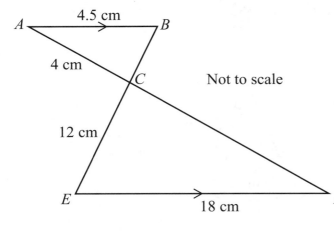

4.5 cm

A

B

4 cm

C

Not to scale

12 cm

E

18 cm

D

a) Find the length of *BC*.

.... cm

[2]

b) Find the length of *AD*.

.... cm

[2]

[Total 4 marks]

5 The quadrilateral *ABCD* is made up of two similar triangles, *ABC* and *ACD*. *AB* = 3 cm,
AD = 8 cm and *AC* = 6 cm. Angle *ABC* = angle *ACD* and angle *ACB* = angle *CAD*.

B

x

C

3 cm

6 cm

Not to scale

y

A

8 cm

D

a) Find the length of sides *x* and *y*.

x = ... cm

y = ... cm

[3]

b) The area of triangle *ABC* is 9 cm². What is the area of quadrilateral *ABCD*?

.... cm²

[2]

[Total 5 marks]

Score:

22

Areas and Perimeters

1   The diagram shows a field in the shape of a trapezium.

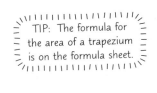

TIP: The formula for the area of a trapezium is on the formula sheet.

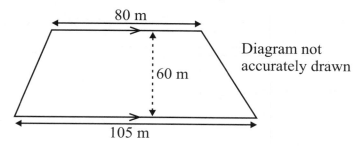

80 m

60 m

105 m

Diagram not accurately drawn

What is the area of the field?

.... m²

[Total 2 marks]

2   Lynn is designing a garden. The diagram shows her design.

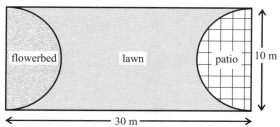

flowerbed   lawn   patio   10 m

30 m

Diagram not accurately drawn

Lynn's garden will be rectangular, with a semicircular flowerbed at one end, and a matching semicircular patio at the other end. The rest of the space will be taken up by a lawn.

a) What will be the area of the lawn in Lynn's garden? Give your answer to 2 d.p.

.... m²

[3]

b) What will be the perimeter of the lawn in Lynn's garden? Give your answer to 2 d.p.

.... m

[3]

[Total 6 marks]

3 The area of the parallelogram shown below is 105 cm².

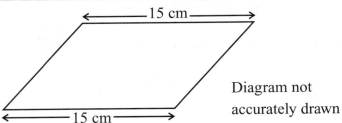

Diagram not
accurately drawn

Calculate the height of the parallelogram.

.... cm

[Total 2 marks]

4 The circle below has a radius of 12 cm.
The sector *S* has a central angle of 50°.

Diagram not
accurately drawn

Find the area of the sector *S* of the circle.
Give your answer to 3 significant figures.

Area of full circle = ... × .... = ...π cm²

Area of sector *S* = ... × area of circle

= .... × .... cm²

= .... cm²

.... cm²

[Total 4 marks]

5 Look at the sector shown in the diagram below. Ⓐ

Diagram not
accurately drawn

30°

6 cm

Find the perimeter of the sector.
Give your answer to 3 significant figures.

Circumference of full circle = ... × .... × .... cm

= .... π cm

Length of arc = ... × circumference of circle

= .... × .... cm = ... cm

Perimeter of sector = ... cm + ... cm + ... cm

= .... cm

.... cm

[Total 4 marks]

Exam Practice Tip

Don't mix up radius and diameter. I know that sounds a bit obvious, but it's something that lots of people do in exams. The radius of a circle is half of its diameter. Think carefully about which one you're being given, and which one you need for a formula.

Score

18

Section Four — Geometry and Measures

Surface Area and Volume

1   The volume of a cube is 729 cm³.

What is the surface area of the cube?

.... cm²
[Total 3 marks]

2   The diagram below shows a cylinder with a diameter of 10 cm and a height of 15 cm.

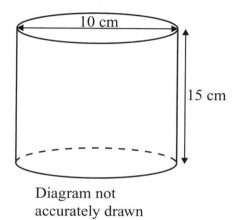

10 cm

15 cm

Diagram not
accurately drawn

a)   What is the surface area of the cylinder?
    Give your answer to 3 significant figures.

.... cm²
[3]

b)   What is the volume of the cylinder?
    Give your answer to 3 significant figures.

.... cm³
[2]

[Total 5 marks]

3   The diagram below shows Amy's new paddling pool.
It has a diameter of 2 metres, and is 40 cm high.

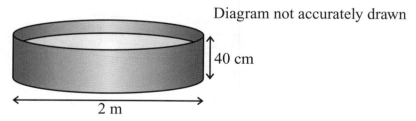

Diagram not accurately drawn

40 cm

2 m

The instructions that came with the pool say that it should only be filled three-quarters full.
What is the maximum volume of water that Amy can put in the pool?
(Give your answer to 2 decimal places.)

.... m³
[Total 3 marks]

Section Four — Geometry and Measures

4   The cross-section of a prism is a regular hexagon.

Each side of the hexagon has a length of 8 cm.
The distance from the centre of the hexagon to
the midpoint of each side is 7 cm.
Calculate the volume of the prism.

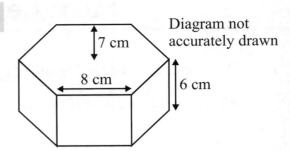

.... cm³

[Total 3 marks]

5   The diagram below shows a wooden spinning top made from a hemisphere and a cone.

The hemisphere has a diameter of 14 cm.
The slanting length of the cone is 12 cm and the radius of its base is 2 cm.

Work out the total surface area of the spinning top.
Give your answer to 3 significant figures.

.... cm²

[Total 4 marks]

6   The diagram below shows a clay bowl in the shape of a hollow hemisphere.
The radius of the inside surface is 8 cm. The radius of the outside surface is 9 cm.

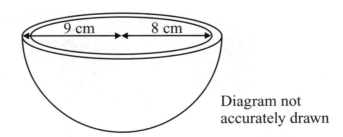

Diagram not
accurately drawn

What volume of clay is needed to make the bowl?
Give your answer to 3 significant figures.

.... cm³

[Total 3 marks]

Section Four — Geometry and Measures

7 The curved surface of a cone is made from the net below.

When the net is folded the cone has a vertical height of 15.5 cm. Calculate the volume of the cone. Give your answer to 3 significant figures.

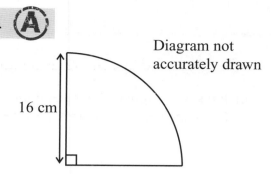

Diagram not accurately drawn

16 cm

.... cm³
[Total 4 marks]

8 The cone and sphere in the diagram below have the same volume.

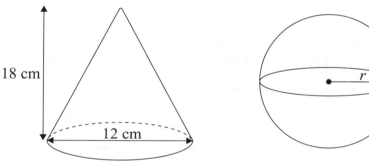

18 cm

12 cm

r

The cone has a vertical height of 18 cm and a base diameter of 12 cm.
Work out the radius, r, of the sphere. Give your answer to 3 significant figures.

.... cm
[Total 4 marks]

9 The diagram shows how two solid spheres fit **exactly** inside a cuboid box.

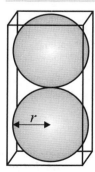

The radius of each sphere is r. Calculate the volume of the space inside the box that is not occupied by the spheres. Give your answer in terms of r and π.

r

....
[Total 3 marks]

Score:

32

Speed

1 Georgina works at a leisure centre which is 6 km from her house. **(D)**

a) It takes Georgina 1 hour and 4 minutes to walk from her house to the leisure centre.
Calculate her average walking speed.

.... km/h
[3]

b) One day Georgina got a lift from her house to the leisure centre.
The average speed of the car was 25 km/h. How long, in minutes, did the journey take?

.... minutes
[3]

[Total 6 marks]

2 John and Alan hired a van. Their receipt gave them information about **(D)**
how much time they spent travelling in the van, and how fast they went.

> Travelling time: 1 hour 15 minutes
> Average Speed: 56 km/h

Calculate the distance that John and Alan travelled in the van.

.... km
[Total 3 marks]

3 In 2013 Mo ran a long-distance race and finished with time, *t*. **(A)**
In 2014 he finished the same race but his time was 10% quicker.

By what percentage did his average speed for the race increase?
Give your answer to 2 decimal places.

Hint: the distance will be
the same for both races.

.... %
[Total 4 marks]

Score:

13

Distance-Time Graphs

1 The distance/time graph below shows Selby's bike ride from his house (**A**) to the zoo (**C**), which is 25 km away.

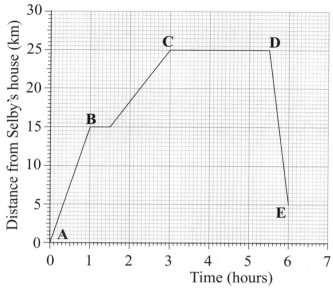

a) After one hour Selby stops at a bench (**B**) to get his breath back.
   Find the gradient of the line between point **A** and point **B**.

   ....

   [2]

b) What does the gradient of the line between point **A** and point **B** represent?

   ....

   [1]

c) How long was Selby's journey to the zoo (**C**) from home (**A**)?

   .... hours

   [1]

d) How long did Selby spend at the zoo?

   .... hours

   [1]

e) After the zoo, Selby stopped at the shops (**E**) for 30 minutes before cycling straight home.
   Given that he arrived home 7 hours after he first left, complete the graph above.

   [2]

f) How many hours did Selby spend cycling in total during the day?

   .... hours

   [1]

   [Total 8 marks]

   Score:

   8

Constructions

1 *EFG* is an isosceles triangle. Sides *EG* and *FG* are both 4.5 cm long.

Side *EF* has been drawn here.

E ——————— F

a) Complete the construction of triangle *EFG* by drawing sides *EG* and *FG*.

[2]

b) Construct the bisector of angle *EGF*.

[2]

[Total 4 marks]

2 *AB* is a straight line.

Use a ruler and compasses to construct the perpendicular bisector of the line *AB*.
Show all of your construction lines.

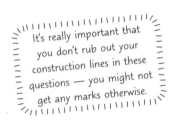

It's really important that you don't rub out your construction lines in these questions — you might not get any marks otherwise.

A
B

[Total 2 marks]

3 *RT* is a straight line with midpoint S.

Use a ruler and compasses to construct an angle of 45° to the line *RST* at the point *S*.
Show all of your construction lines.

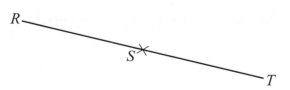

R
S
T

[Total 4 marks]

4   A kite *ABCD* sides *AB* and *CB* are both 6 cm long
    and sides *AD* and *CD* are both 9 cm long.
    The shorter diagonal of the kite, *AC*, has a length of 8 cm.

Construct an accurate, full-size drawing of the kite and label the corners.
Show all your construction lines.

A ——————————————————————— C

[Total 4 marks]

Exam Practice Tip

Always draw your construction lines as accurately as possible — make sure your compass is set to the
correct length before you draw each arc. You can check the accuracy of your construction at the end
by measuring the length of the sides with a ruler or the size of an angles with a protractor.

Score

14

Section Four — Geometry and Measures

Pythagoras' Theorem

1 The diagram shows a right-angled triangle *ABC*.
AC is 4 cm long. *BC* is 8 cm long.

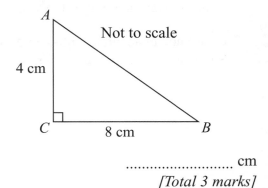

Calculate the length of *AB*.
Give your answer to 2 decimal places.

.... cm
[Total 3 marks]

2 A ladder is 3.5 m long. For safety, when the ladder is leant against a wall,
the base should never be less than 2.1 m away from the wall.

What is the maximum vertical height that the top of the ladder can safely reach to?

.... m
[Total 3 marks]

3 A triangle has a base of 10 cm. Its other two sides are both 13 cm long.

Calculate the area of the triangle.

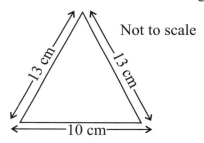

.... cm²
[Total 4 marks]

4 The diagram shows a kite *ABCD*. *AB* is 28.3 cm long.
BC is 54.3 cm long. *BE* is 20 cm in length.

Work out the perimeter of triangle *ABC*. Give your answer to 1 decimal place.

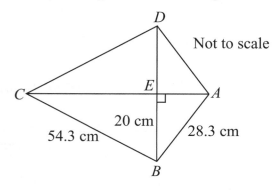

.... cm
[Total 5 marks]

Score:
15

Trigonometry — Sin, Cos, Tan

1 The diagram shows a right-angled triangle.

Find the size of the angle marked x.
Give your answer to 1 decimal place.

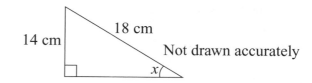

.... °

[Total 3 marks]

2 The diagram shows a right-angled triangle.

Find the length of the side marked y.
Give your answer to 3 significant figures.

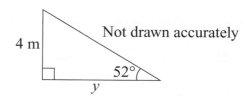

.... m
[Total 3 marks]

3 In the triangle below, $AB = BC = 10$ m and angle $C = 34°$.

a) Calculate the length AC.
   Give your answer to 2 decimal places.

.... m
[3]

b) Calculate the height of the triangle.
   Give your answer to 2 decimal places.

.... m
[3]

[Total 6 marks]

Section Five — Pythagoras and Trigonometry

4 *X*, *Y* and *Z* are points on a circle, where *XY* is a diameter of the circle.

Calculate the length of *YZ*, giving your answer correct to 2 decimal places.

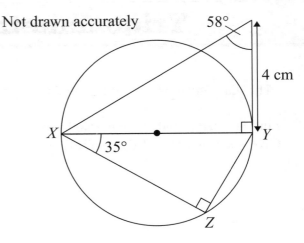

Not drawn accurately

.... cm

[Total 4 marks]

5 The diagram shows a kite *EFGH*.
Diagonal *EG* bisects the diagonal *HF* at *M*.
EM = 5 cm, *MG* = 9 cm and *HF* = 12 cm.

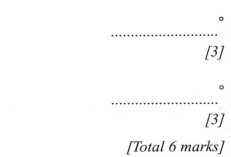

Not drawn accurately

a) Calculate the size of angle *FGM*.
   Give your answer to 1 decimal place.

.............................°

[3]

b) Calculate the size of angle *FEH*.
   Give your answer to 1 decimal place.

.............................°

[3]

[Total 6 marks]

6 A regular hexagon is drawn such that all of its vertices are on the circumference of a circle of radius 8.5 cm.

Calculate the distance from the centre of the circle to the centre of one edge of the hexagon.
Give your answer to 2 decimal places.

The sum of internal angles in a polygon
= (number of sides − 2) × 180°

.... cm

[Total 5 marks]

Exam Practice Tip

In an exam, it'll help if you start by labelling the sides of a right-angled triangle, opposite (O), adjacent (A) and hypotenuse (H) — these are easy to get muddled up. If you're working out an angle, make sure you check whether it's sensible — if you get an angle of 720° or 0.0072°, it's probably wrong so give it another go.

Score

27

The Sine and Cosine Rules

1   In the triangle below, AB = 10 cm, BC = 7 cm and angle ABC = 85°.

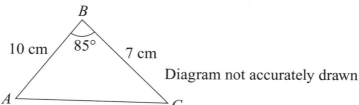

Diagram not accurately drawn

a) Calculate the length of AC.
   Give your answer to 3 significant figures.

AC^2 = ...^{2} + ...^{2} − (2 × .... × .... × cos ....°)

$AC = \sqrt{\text{............} - \text{............} \times \cos \text{............}^{\circ}}$

AC = ...

.... cm
[3]

b) Calculate the area of triangle ABC.
   Give your answer to 3 significant figures.

.... cm²
[2]

[Total 5 marks]

2   The diagram below is a sketch of a metal framework.
     Some of the information needed to manufacture the framework has been lost.

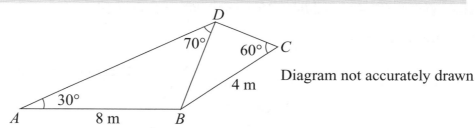

Diagram not accurately drawn

Complete the specification for the framework by calculating:

a) the length of BD.
   Give your answer to 3 significant figures.

$$\frac{BD}{\sin \text{............}} = \frac{\text{............}}{\sin \text{............}}$$

$$BD = \frac{\text{............}}{\sin \text{............}} \times \sin \text{............}$$

BD = ... m

.... m
[3]

b) the size of angle BDC.
   Give your answer to 3 significant figures.

.... °
[3]

[Total 6 marks]

Section Five — Pythagoras and Trigonometry

72

3   A castle drawbridge is supported by two chains, *AB* and *AC*. Using the information on the diagram, calculate the total length of the drawbridge, *BD*, correct to 3 s.f.

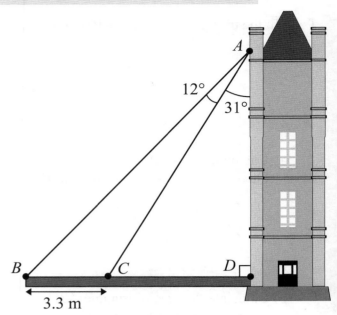

.... m

[Total 6 marks]

4   In the triangle below, *AB* = 12 cm, *BC* = 19 cm and *AC* = 14 cm.

Calculate the area of the triangle.

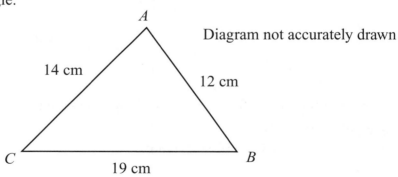

Diagram not accurately drawn

.... cm²

[Total 5 marks]

5   *ABCD* is a quadrilateral.

$AB = 55$ cm.
$DC = 84$ cm.
Angle $ABC = 116°$.
Angle $BCD = 78°$.

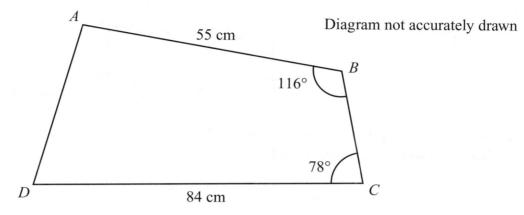

Diagram not accurately drawn

Given that $AC = 93$ cm, work out the area of *ABCD* to 3 significant figures.
Show clearly how you get your answer.

.... cm^2
[Total 8 marks]

Score:

30

Section Five — Pythagoras and Trigonometry

3D Pythagoras and Trigonometry

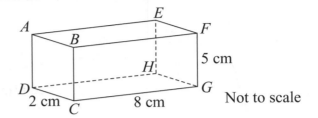

a) Sam is collecting sticks. Work out the length of the longest stick that he can fit into the box.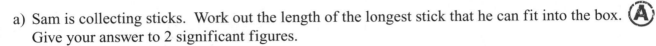
Give your answer to 2 significant figures.

..........................… cm

[3]

b) A straight stick is placed in the box and wedged between points *F* and *D*. Ⓐ*
Find the size of the angle the stick makes with the line *DG*.
Give your answer to 2 significant figures.

..........................… °

[2]

[Total 5 marks]

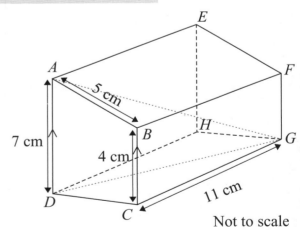

..........................… °

[Total 5 marks]

Score:

10

Section Five — Pythagoras and Trigonometry

Vectors

1 ABCD is a parallelogram. $\overrightarrow{AB} = 2\mathbf{a}$ and $\overrightarrow{AD} = 2\mathbf{d}$.
L is the midpoint of AC, and M is the midpoint of BC.

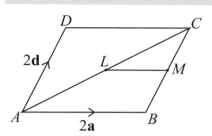

Not drawn accurately

Write in terms of **a** and **d**:

a) $\overrightarrow{CD}$

....

[1]

b) $\overrightarrow{AC}$

....

[1]

c) $\overrightarrow{BL}$

....

[1]

[Total 3 marks]

2 In the diagram, $\overrightarrow{OA} = 2\mathbf{a}$ and $\overrightarrow{OB} = \mathbf{b}$.
M is the midpoint of AB.

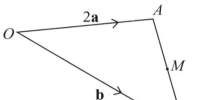

Not drawn accurately

a) Find $\overrightarrow{OM}$ in terms of **a** and **b**.

$$\overrightarrow{OM} = \underline{\hspace{1cm}} + \underline{\hspace{1cm}} = \underline{\hspace{1cm}} + \frac{1}{2}\underline{\hspace{1cm}}$$

$$\overrightarrow{AB} = \underline{\hspace{0.5cm}} + \underline{\hspace{0.5cm}}$$

$$\overrightarrow{OM} = \underline{\hspace{0.5cm}} + \frac{1}{2}(\underline{\hspace{2cm}}) = \underline{\hspace{2cm}}$$

X is a point on AB such that $AX:XB = 1:3$.
b) Find $\overrightarrow{OX}$ in terms of **a** and **b**.

....

[2]

....

[2]

[Total 4 marks]

3 ABCD is a parallelogram. $\overrightarrow{AB} = 3\mathbf{a}$ and $\overrightarrow{BW} = \mathbf{b}$.

M is the midpoint of CD and $AX = 2XC$.
$BW:WC = 1:5$

a) Find $\overrightarrow{BX}$ in terms of **a** and **b**.

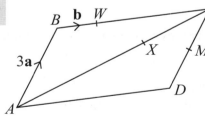

Not drawn accurately

....

[3]

b) Hence show that B, X and M are three points on a straight line.

[2]

[Total 5 marks]

Score: ☐

12

 ☐   ☐   ☐

Section Five — Pythagoras and Trigonometry

Mean, Median, Mode and Range

1   Sam thinks of three different whole numbers. **(E)**

The numbers have a range of 6 and a mean of 4.
What are the three numbers?

..................., ..., ...

[Total 2 marks]

2   15 boys and 13 girls took a Maths test. The mean mark for the boys was b.
In the same test the mean mark for the girls was g.
Write down an expression for the mean mark of all 28 pupils. **(D)**

....

[Total 3 marks]

3   Declan is training to take part in a 10 km race. **(C)**
He runs the same distance every day for 30 days.

For the first 20 days, his mean running time was 56.2 minutes.
His mean running time for all 30 days was 54.4 minutes.

Work out Declan's mean running time for the last 10 days of his training.

    Total running time for first 20 days = 20 × .... = ...

    Total running time for all 30 days = ... × .... = ...

    Total running time for last 10 days = ... − .... = ...

    Mean running time for last 10 days = ... ÷ ....

.... minutes

[Total 4 marks]

4   Lee has 6 pygmy goats. Their weights, in kg, are listed below. **(C)**

       32   23   31   28   36   26

Two of the goats wander off and don't return. The remaining 4 goats have a mean
weight of the 27.25 kg. Find the weights of the two goats who wandered off.

.... kg and .... kg

[Total 4 marks]

Score: ⬜

13

Quartiles and Comparing Distributions

1   Liz sells earrings. The prices in pounds of 15 pairs of earrings are given below. **B**

  6   3   4   8   10   11   5   7   4   12   8   9   5   7   11

a) Find the lower and upper quartiles of the prices above.

> Start by writing the prices in ascending order.

Lower quartile = ...   Upper quartile = ...

[2]

b) Liz reduces all her prices by 50p. Will the interquartile range of the new prices be less than, greater than or the same as the interquartile range of the old prices? Give a reason for your answer.

....

....

[1]

[Total 3 marks]

2   The data below shows the number of strawberries collected from each plant during one harvest of two strawberry patches. **B**

| Patch A: | 8 | 13 | 19 | 22 | 8 | 18 | 14 | 16 | 9 | 14 | 12 |
| Patch B: | 14 | 19 | 11 | 13 | 15 | 11 | 13 | | | | |

a) For each patch, work out the interquartile range for the number of strawberries from each plant.

Patch A: ....   Patch B: ....

[4]

b) Give one comparison between the plants in Patch A and the plants in Patch B, based on your results in part a).

....

....

[1]

[Total 5 marks]

Score: ☐

8

Frequency Tables — Finding Averages

1 The table shows the number of pets owned by each of the 29 pupils in class 7F.

Number of pets	Frequency
0	8
1	3
2	5
3	8
4	4
5	1

a) Find the total number of pets owned by pupils in class 7F.

....

[2]

b) Work out the mean number of pets per pupil in class 7F.

....

[2]

[Total 4 marks]

2 For her homework, Vanessa collected information about the number of text messages that 36 pupils in her school sent one day. She recorded her results in the frequency table below.

Number of messages	Frequency
0	2
2	4
3	7
5	11
7	6
8	3
10	3
Total	36

Use the table to calculate the mean number of text messages sent.

....

[Total 3 marks]

Score:

7

Grouped Frequency Tables

1   The table shows the time it took 32 pupils to run a 200 m sprint.

Time (t seconds)	Frequency
$22 < t \le 26$	4
$26 < t \le 30$	8
$30 < t \le 34$	13
$34 < t \le 38$	6
$38 < t \le 42$	1

a) All pupils with a time of 30 seconds or less qualified for the next round.
What percentage of pupils did not qualify for the next round?

.........................%

[2]

b) Estimate how long it would take the four quickest runners to run a
4 × 200 m relay race (where they each run 200 m one after the other).

.... seconds

[2]

[Total 4 marks]

2   The grouped frequency table below shows the number of hours of exercise 44 adults did in one week.

Hours of exercise (x)	Frequency
$0 \le x < 2$	15
$2 \le x < 4$	9
$4 \le x < 6$	8
$6 \le x < 8$	6
$8 \le x < 10$	3
$10 \le x < 12$	3

Work out an estimate for the total time spent exercising by the 44 adults that week.

.... hours

[Total 3 marks]

3 32 pupils in a class sat an exam in Science.
The distribution of their marks is given in the table below.

Exam mark	Frequency
$10 < x \le 20$	2
$20 < x \le 30$	5
$30 < x \le 40$	7
$40 < x \le 50$	8
$50 < x \le 60$	4
$60 < x \le 70$	6

Use the table to find:

a) the modal class.

....
[1]

b) an estimate of the mean (give your answer to 3 s.f.).

Tip: add a couple of columns to the table to help you.

.... marks
[4]

[Total 5 marks]

4 During a science experiment 10 seeds were planted and their growth was measured in cm after 12 days. The results were recorded in the table below.

Growth in cm	Number of plants
$0 \le x \le 2$	2
$3 \le x \le 5$	4
$6 \le x \le 8$	3
$9 \le x \le 11$	1

a) Use the table to find an estimate of the mean growth.

.... cm
[4]

b) Explain why you can only find an estimate of the mean.

....

....
[1]

[Total 5 marks]

Score:

17

Section Six — Statistics and Probability

Cumulative Frequency

1   120 pupils in a year group sit an examination at the end of the year. Their results are given in the table below.

Exam mark (%)	$0 < x \leq 20$	$20 < x \leq 30$	$30 < x \leq 40$	$40 < x \leq 50$	$50 < x \leq 60$	$60 < x \leq 70$	$70 < x \leq 80$	$80 < x \leq 100$
Frequency	3	10	12	24	42	16	9	4

a) Complete the cumulative frequency table below.

Exam mark (%)	≤ 20	≤ 30	≤ 40	≤ 50	≤ 60	≤ 70	≤ 80	≤ 100
Cumulative Frequency								

[1]

b) Use your table to draw a cumulative frequency graph on the graph paper.

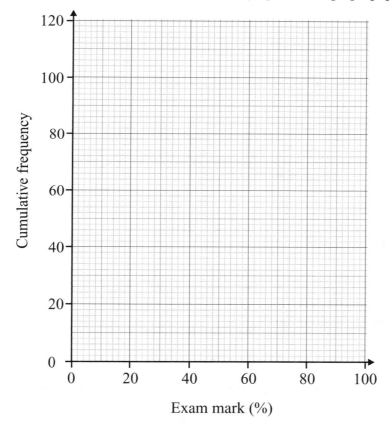

[2]

c) Use your graph to find an estimate for the median.

.... %

[1]

d) Use your graph to find an estimate for the inter-quartile range.

.... %

[2]

[Total 6 marks]

Section Six — Statistics and Probability

2   The cumulative frequency table below gives information about the length of time it takes to travel between Udderston and Trundle on the main road each morning.

Journey Time (t mins)	$0 < t \leq 20$	$0 < t \leq 25$	$0 < t \leq 30$	$0 < t \leq 35$	$0 < t \leq 45$	$0 < t \leq 60$
Cumulative Frequency	7	22	36	45	49	50

a) On the graph paper below, draw a cumulative frequency graph for the table.

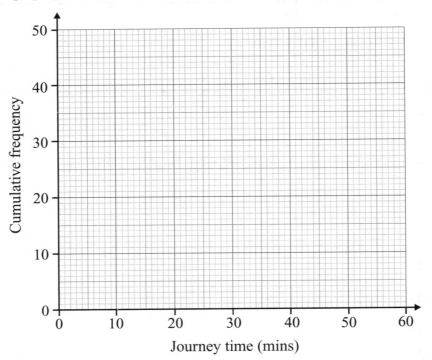

[2]

b) Use your graph to estimate the number of journeys that took between 27 and 47 minutes.

.... journeys

[2]

c) Use your graph to estimate the percentage of journeys that took longer than 40 minutes.

.... %

[2]

The median time for an evening journey from Udderston to Trundle is 22 minutes.

d) Give one comparison of the morning and evening journey times from Udderston to Trundle.

....

....

[2]

[Total 8 marks]

Score:

14

Section Six — Statistics and Probability

Histograms and Frequency Density

1   The histogram shows the number of minutes some pupils watched television for one evening.

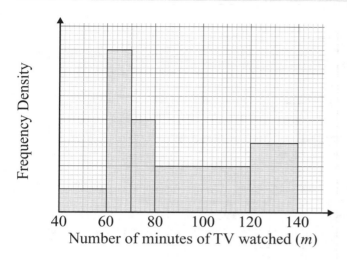

Number of minutes of TV watched (m)	Frequency
$40 \leq m < 60$	20
$60 \leq m < 70$	
$70 \leq m < 80$	
$80 \leq m < 120$	
$120 \leq m < 140$	

Use the histogram to complete the frequency table.

Start by finding the frequency density for the first interval.

[Total 2 marks]

2   100 Year 11 pupils were each given a potato. The table below gives some information about how long it took the pupils to peel their potato. Use the information in the table to draw a histogram on the grid below.

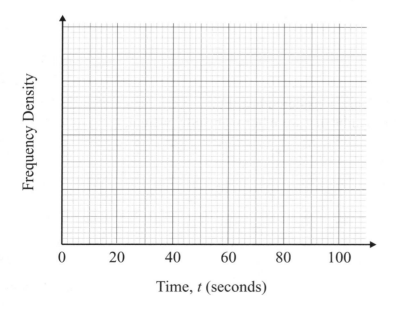

Time, t (s)	Frequency
$0 < t \leq 20$	15
$20 < t \leq 30$	35
$30 < t \leq 40$	30
$40 < t \leq 60$	15
$60 < t \leq 100$	5

[Total 3 marks]

Section Six — Statistics and Probability

3 The histogram shows the weights, w kg, of some newborn lambs. All the lambs weighed between 2 kg and 6 kg.

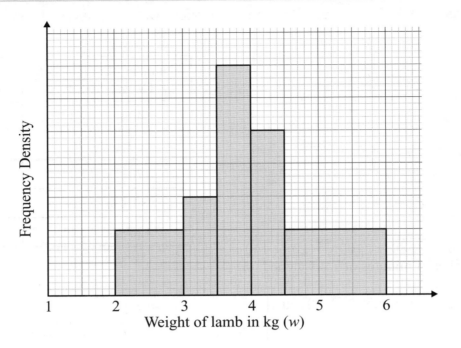

a) What percentage of the lambs weighed less than 3.5 kg?

.... %

[3]

b) 45 lambs weighed between 4 kg and 4.5 kg.
   What was the total number of lambs that were weighed?

....

[2]

c) Lambs with a weight greater than 3.2 kg are considered healthy.
   Calculate an estimate of the number of lambs that were born a healthy weight.

....

[3]

[Total 8 marks]

Score:

13

Section Six — Statistics and Probability

Probability Basics

1 Amelie takes some photos of her sister.
The probability that her sister will be blinking in a photo is $\frac{2}{5}$.

Amelie picks one photo at random.
What is the probability that her sister is not blinking in the photo?

....
[Total 2 marks]

2 There are 10 counters in a bag.
Four of the counters are blue and the rest are red.
One counter is picked out at random.

a) Work out the probability that the counter picked is red.
Give your answer as a fraction in its lowest terms.

....
[2]

b) What is the probability that the counter picked is green?

....
[1]
[Total 3 marks]

3 Arthur has stripy, spotty and plain socks in his drawer.
He picks a sock from the drawer at random.

The probability that he picks a plain sock is 0.4.
He is twice as likely to pick a stripy sock than a spotty sock.
What is the probability that he picks a spotty sock? Give your answer as a decimal.

let P(spotty sock) = y

then P(stripy sock) = ... y

.... + y + ... = 1

.... = 0.6

y = ...

....
[Total 4 marks]

Score: [ ]

9

 [ ]   [ ]   [ ]

Expected Frequency

1   A fair spinner has 8 sections coloured red, blue and green. 2 of the sections are coloured red, 3 are coloured blue and the rest are coloured green.

If the spinner is spun 200 times, how many times would you except it to land on green?

....
[Total 3 marks]

2   The total number of pupils in a school is 834.

Work out an estimate for the number of pupils who were born on a Tuesday.

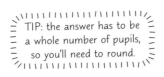
TIP: the answer has to be
a whole number of pupils,
so you'll need to round.

.... pupils
[Total 4 marks]

3   Shaun is playing the game 'hook-a-duck'.

The base of each rubber duck is numbered either 1, 2, 3, 4 or 5. The table below shows the probability of a randomly chosen duck being labelled with each number.

Number	1	2	3	4	5
Probability	0.18	0.36		0.19	0.06

a) Complete the table by finding the probability that Shaun will hook a duck numbered 3.

[1]

You win the game by hooking a duck numbered 2.
b) Shaun plays the game 50 times. Estimate how many times he does **not** win.

....
[3]

[Total 4 marks]

Score:

11

Section Six — Statistics and Probability

The AND / OR Rules

1   Here is a 5-sided spinner.
    The spinner is biased.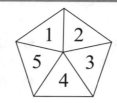

The probability that the spinner will land on the numbers 1 to 4 is given in this table.

Number	1	2	3	4	5
Probability	0.3	0.15	0.2	0.25	

I spin the spinner once.

a) Work out the probability the spinner will not land on 2.

....

[2]

b) Work out the probability the spinner will land on an odd number.

....

[3]

c) Work out the probability that the spinner will land on 5.

....

[2]

I spin the spinner twice.

d) Work out the probability that the spinner will land on 3 both times.

....

[2]

[Total 9 marks]

2   A biscuit tin contains 13 normal digestives and 7 chocolate digestives.
    Jimmy chooses two biscuits at random from the tin without replacement.

a) What is the probability that Jimmy will choose two chocolate digestives?
   Give your answer as a fraction in its simplest form.

TIP: this is *without replacement*,
so the total number of biscuits in
the tin goes down each time.

....

[3]

b) Work out the probability that Jimmy chooses one normal and one chocolate digestive.
   Give your answer as a fraction in its simplest form.

....

[3]

[Total 6 marks]

Section Six — Statistics and Probability

3 Josie has six different cards, shown below. (A)

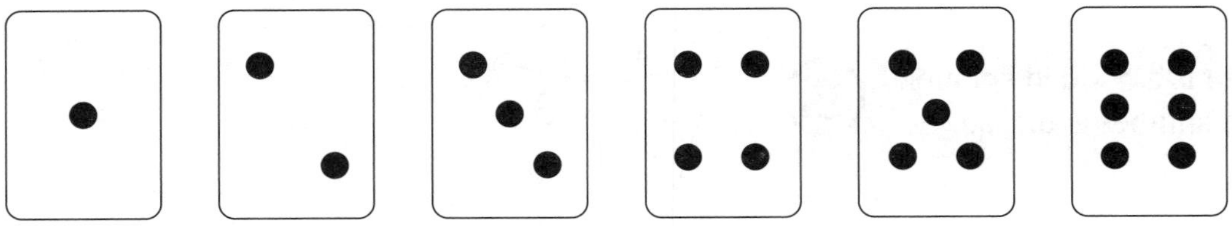

a) Find the probability that a randomly chosen card will have fewer than 3 dots on it.

....
[2]

b) Josie picks a card, replaces it and picks another card.
What is the probability that the total number of dots on the two cards will be 4?

....
[3]

c) Josie picks another two cards at random, but this time she does **not** replace them.
What is the probability that the total number of dots on the two cards will be greater than 9?

....
[3]

[Total 8 marks]

4 Rebecca buys a bag of beads to make a necklace. (A*)
The bag contains 8 brown beads and 12 orange beads.
She picks three beads from the bag and puts them onto a string.

Work out the probability that she puts 2 orange beads and one brown bead onto her string, in **any** order.

....
[Total 3 marks]

Exam Practice Tip

All you need to remember here is if you're being asked the probability of Thing One AND Thing Two happening you MULTIPLY, and if you're being asked the probability of Thing One OR Thing Two happening you ADD. Careful with your adding and multiplying if your probabilities are fractions — it's an easy way to slip up.

Score

26

Tree Diagrams

1 Jo and Heather are meeting for coffee.
The probability that Jo will wear burgundy trousers is $\frac{2}{5}$.
There is a one in four chance that Heather will wear burgundy trousers.
The two events are independent.

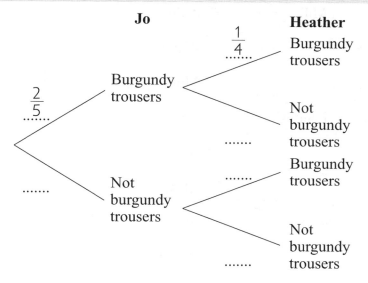

a) Complete the tree diagram above. *[2]*

b) What is the probability that neither of them wear burgundy trousers?

Probability neither wear burgundy trousers = $\frac{3}{5} \times \frac{......}{......} = \frac{......}{......}$ ....

[2]

[Total 4 marks]

2 A couple are both carriers of a recessive gene that causes a hereditary disease.
If they have a child, the probability that the child will suffer from the disease is 0.25.
The couple plan to have two children.

If the couple have two children, find the probability that at least one of them will have the disease.

....

[Total 5 marks]

90

3   A box of chocolates contains 12 chocolates.
5 of the chocolates are milk chocolate, 4 are plain chocolate and 3 are white chocolate.
Two chocolates are chosen at random without replacement.

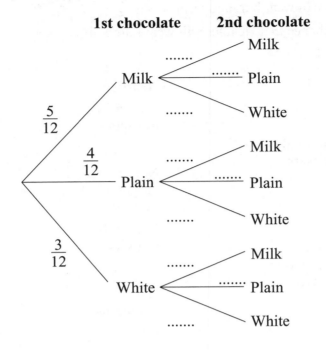

a) Complete the tree diagram above.

[2]

b) Calculate the probability that one milk chocolate and one white chocolate are chosen.

....

[3]

c) Work out the probability that at least one plain chocolate is chosen.

....

[3]

[Total 8 marks]

Score:

17

Candidate Surname		Candidate Forename(s)

Centre Number	Candidate Number	Candidate Signature

Edexcel International GCSE

Mathematics
Paper 3H

Higher Tier

Practice Paper
Time allowed: 2 hours

You must have:
Pen, pencil, eraser, ruler, protractor, pair of compasses.
You may use tracing paper.

You **may use** a calculator.

Instructions to candidates
- Use **black** ink to write your answers.
- Write your name and other details in the spaces provided above.
- Answer **all** questions in the spaces provided.
- Correct answers without sufficient working might not be awarded any marks.
- Do all rough work on the paper.
- Anything you write on the formula sheet will **not** gain any credit.

Information for candidates
- The marks available are given in brackets at the end of each question.
- There are 25 questions in this paper. There are no blank pages.
- There are 100 marks available for this paper.

Get the answers online
Your free Online Edition of this book includes worked solutions for this Exam Paper,
which you can print out or view on screen.
There's more info about how to get your Online Edition at the front of this book.

Answer ALL the questions.

Write your answers in the spaces provided.

You must show all of your working.

1   The shape below is an irregular hexagon.

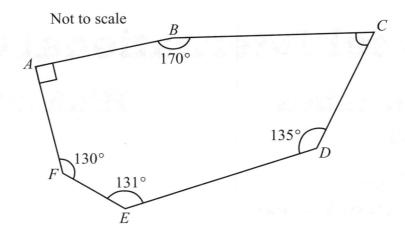

(a)   What is the sum of the interior angles of a hexagon?

..........................°

[2]

(b)   Work out the size of angle *BCD*.

..........................°

[2]

[Total 4 marks]

2   Arthur thinks of three different positive whole numbers.
    The numbers have a range of 6 and a mean of 9. What are the three numbers?

..............., ..., ...

[Total 2 marks]

3 Last year a bookshop sold 9000 books.
Three-quarters of all the books sold were fiction.
The rest were autobiographies and revision guides in the ratio 7 : 3.

How many revision guides were sold?

....

[Total 3 marks]

4 Katie's journey to work from home is 60 km in length, and the journey takes 40 minutes.
Work out Katie's average speed in km/h.

.... km/h

[Total 3 marks]

5 Adam is a car salesman with an annual salary of £20 000.
He also gets paid commission of 3% on any sales that he makes.
Last year his average monthly sales were £20 500.

What percentage of his total income was from his salary? Give your answer to 2 decimal places.

.... %

[Total 3 marks]

6 Factorise the following expressions fully.

(a) $9x + 6$

....

[1]

(b) $8y^3 + 4y$

....

[2]

(c) $25a^2 - b^2$

....

[2]

[Total 5 marks]

---

7 Write 56^2 as a product of its prime factors.

....

[Total 3 marks]

3

8   The shape below is a kite made up of three triangles.

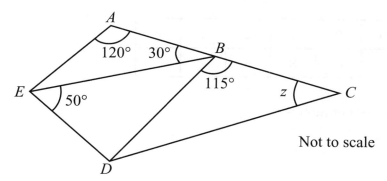

Not to scale

Work out the size of angle *z*.

.... °

[Total 3 marks]

9   A sweet shop sells cylindrical tubs of sherbet.
The cylindrical tubs have an internal diameter of 3.8 cm and are 4.9 cm tall.

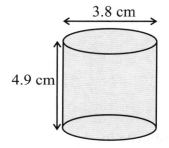

Diagram not
accurately drawn

1 cm³ of sherbet weighs 0.63 g.

Calculate the weight, in grams, of sherbet in a full tub.
Give your answer correct to 2 decimal places.

.... g

[Total 3 marks]

4

Practice Paper 1

10   A traffic survey at a road junction recorded the following numbers of vehicles arriving per minute.

Vehicles per minute	0	1	2	3	4
Frequency	13	8	6	2	1

What is the mean number of vehicles per minute?

....

[Total 3 marks]

---

11   Jack gets an even number 55 times when he rolls a biased dice 80 times.

(a)   Find an estimate for the probability that the
next time Jack rolls the dice, he'll get an odd number.

....

[2]

(b)   Meg rolls the same dice 240 times. Find an estimate for the
number of times she gets an even number.

....

[2]

[Total 4 marks]

5

12 (a) Find the equation of the line shown below.
Give your answer in the form $ax + by + c = 0$, where a, b and c are integers.

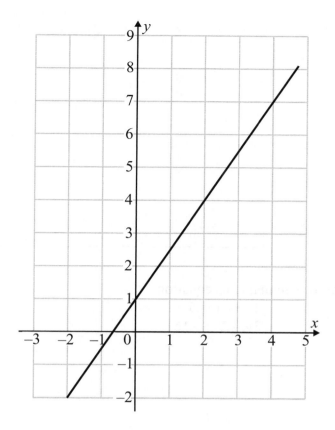

....
[3]

(b) Find the equation of the line that is parallel to the line $y = 4x - 2$
and passes through the point (8, 1).

....
[2]

[Total 5 marks]

6

13 Rearrange the equations below to make b the subject in each case.

(a) $a = \dfrac{1}{2}bc^2$

....
[2]

(b) $12 = \dfrac{bx + 8}{by - 4}$

....
[3]

[Total 5 marks]

---

14 Solve the following pair of simultaneous equations.
$$3x + 5y = 5$$
$$3y - 2x = -16$$

$x =$ .... $y =$ ....

[Total 4 marks]

7

15 (a) Simplify

(i) $m^4 \times m^3$

....

(ii) $(8n^6)^{\frac{1}{3}}$

....
[3]

(b) Expand and simplify $(p-3)(p+5)$

....
[2]

(c) Solve $8(2q-4) + 5(q+11) = 65$

$q =$ ....
[3]

[Total 8 marks]

16 Write $0.1\dot{5}$ as a fraction. Simplify your answer as far as possible.

....
[Total 2 marks]

17 The distance from London to New York is 5600 km to the nearest 100 km.

   (a) Write down the shortest possible distance between the two cities.

                                                .... km

                                                                          [1]

   (b) Calculate the longest possible distance for a trip from London to New York and back again.

                                                .... km

                                                                          [2]

                                                                          [Total 3 marks]

18 The diagram below shows pyramid *PQRST*.

    PR is 8.5 cm and the diagonal *RT* is 10 cm.

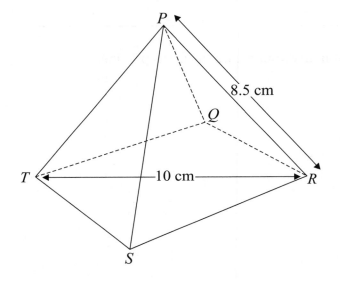

                                                         Diagram not accurately drawn

The plane *PRT* has an area of 35 cm².

Calculate the size of angle *PRT*. Give your answer correct to 1 decimal place.

                                                                          °

                                                      ....

                                                                          [Total 4 marks]

Practice Paper 1

19 Simplify these algebraic fractions as much as possible.

(a) $\dfrac{4x + 10}{6x + 14}$

....

[2]

(b) $\dfrac{x^2 - 2x - 15}{x^2 + 10x + 21}$

....

[3]

[Total 5 marks]

20 Calculate the area of the shaded segment in the diagram below.
Give your answer to 2 decimal places.

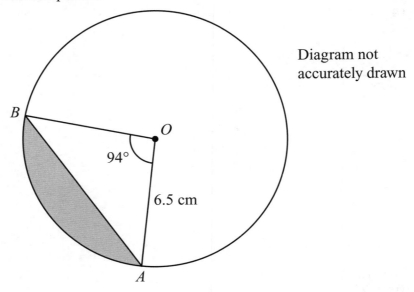

Diagram not
accurately drawn

.... cm²

[Total 6 marks]

11

Practice Paper 1

21 At a school canteen, the probability of chips being served on any day is 0.2.
On a day when chips are served, the probability of the canteen having ketchup is 0.4.
On a day when chips are not served, the canteen is twice as likely to have ketchup
as on a day when chips are served.

On a randomly selected day, what is the probability that the canteen will have ketchup?

....

[Total 4 marks]

22   The histogram below shows information about the length of time
100 cars were parked in a supermarket car park.

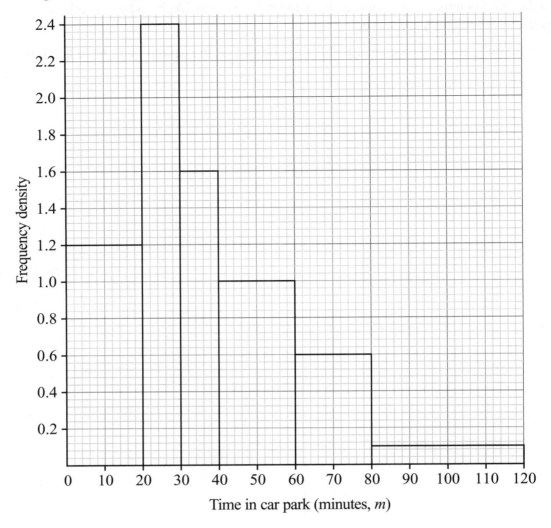

(a)   Estimate how many cars were parked for more than 70 minutes.

....

[2]

(b)   Calculate an estimate of the mean length of time the cars were parked for.

.... minutes

[3]

[Total 5 marks]

Practice Paper 1

23 In the diagram below, O is the centre of the circle.
    A, B, C and D are all points on the circumference of the circle, and DE and BE are tangents.
    Angle DAB is 100°.

    Find the size of angle DEB. Give a reason for each stage of your working.

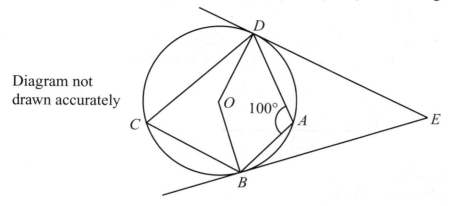

Diagram not
drawn accurately

....................°

[Total 4 marks]

24 The expression $\dfrac{\sqrt{72} + 6}{\sqrt{2}}$ can be simplified to $a + b\sqrt{2}$, where a and b are integers.

    Find the values of a and b.

$a =$ .... $b =$ ....

[Total 3 marks]

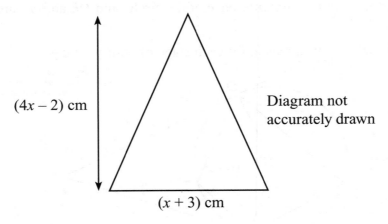

$(4x - 2)$ cm

Diagram not accurately drawn

$(x + 3)$ cm

The diagram shows a triangle.
The height of the triangle is $(4x - 2)$ cm.
The base length of the triangle is $(x + 3)$ cm.
The area of the triangle is 43 cm².

(a) Show that $2x^2 + 5x - 46 = 0$.

[3]

(b) Find the value of x correct to 3 significant figures.
      Show all your working clearly.

....

[3]

[Total 6 marks]

[TOTAL FOR PAPER = 100 MARKS]

Practice Paper 1

Candidate Surname	Candidate Forename(s)

Centre Number	Candidate Number	Candidate Signature

Edexcel International GCSE

Mathematics
Paper 4H

Higher Tier

Practice Paper
Time allowed: 2 hours

You must have:
Pen, pencil, eraser, ruler, protractor, pair of compasses.
You may use tracing paper.

You may use a calculator.

Instructions to candidates
- Use **black** ink to write your answers.
- Write your name and other details in the spaces provided above.
- Answer **all** questions in the spaces provided.
- Correct answers without sufficient working might not be awarded any marks.
- Do all rough work on the paper.
- Anything you write on the formula sheet will **not** gain any credit.

Information for candidates
- The marks available are given in brackets at the end of each question.
- There are 21 questions in this paper. There are no blank pages.
- There are 100 marks available for this paper.

Get the answers online

Your free Online Edition of this book includes worked solutions for this Exam Paper,
which you can print out or view on screen.
There's more info about how to get your Online Edition at the front of this book.

Answer ALL the questions.

Write your answers in the spaces provided.

You must show all of your working.

1   In a class of 26 children, 12 are boys and the rest are girls.

(a)   Work out the ratio of boys to girls.
Give your answer in its simplest form.

....

[2]

In another class the ratio of boys to girls is $2:3$.
There are 25 children in the class.

(b)   Work out how many girls are in the class.

.... girls

[2]

[Total 4 marks]

2   Use your calculator to work out $\sqrt{\dfrac{79.7 \times 7.9}{\sin 80° + 1}}$

(a)   Write down all the figures on your calculator display.

....

[2]

(b)   Write down your answer to part (a) correct to 3 significant figures.

....

[1]

[Total 3 marks]

1

Practice Paper 2

3   Alice walks to the garage to pick up her car.
Her journey is shown on the distance-time graph below.

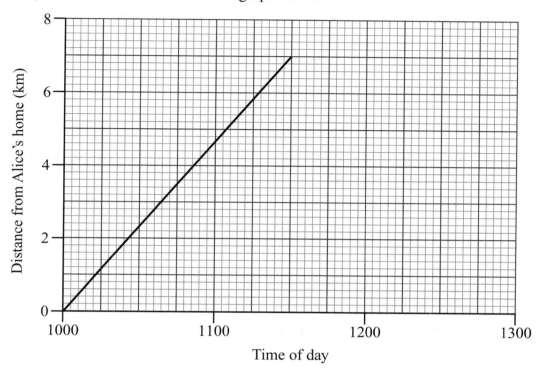

(a)   How far is it from Alice's house to the garage?

.... km

[1]

(b)   At what speed does she walk to the garage? Give your answer to 2 d.p.

.... km/h

[3]

Alice spends 30 minutes at the garage, then drives home at a constant speed.
She arrives home at 1218.

(c)   Complete the graph to show the time that Alice spends at the garage and her return journey.

[2]

(d)   How long was Alice away from home for in total?

....

[1]

[Total 7 marks]

2

4   Aled wants to buy a suitcase to take on holiday.
He sees a suitcase which was £18, but today it has 10% off.

(a)   How much money would he get off the suitcase if he bought it today?

£
[2]

He sees another suitcase which was £24, but the ticket says today the price is reduced by £6.

(b)   What is £6 as a percentage of £24?

.... %
[2]

[Total 4 marks]

---

5   (a)   Write down the integer values satisfying the inequality $-2 \leq b < 3$.

[2]

(b)   On the number line below, plot the range of numbers which satisfy the
inequality $2a - 1 < 7a - 16$.

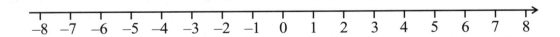

[3]

[Total 5 marks]

6 The table below gives information about the heights of the children in Class A.

Height in cm (h)	Frequency
$130 \leq h < 140$	5
$140 \leq h < 150$	10
$150 \leq h < 160$	14
$160 \leq h < 170$	8
$170 \leq h < 180$	3

Calculate an estimate for the mean height of the children in Class A.

.... cm

[Total 4 marks]

7 On the grid below, shade the region that satisfies all three of these inequalities:

$$x \leq 3 \qquad y > -4 \qquad y \leq x + 2$$

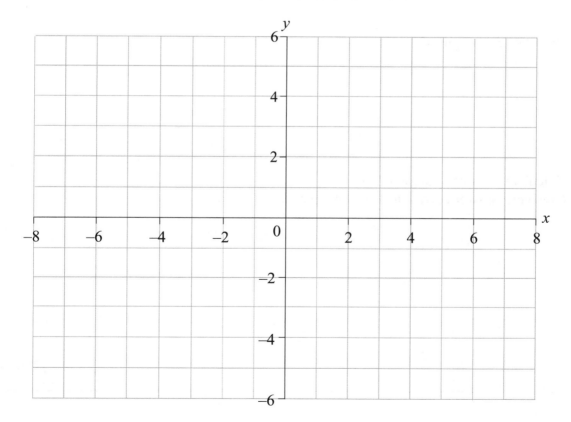

[Total 4 marks]

4

Practice Paper 2

8   In February 2010, the UK population was estimated to be 62 000 000 people.

The UK national debt is the money that the UK government owes to people who have bought government bonds. In February 2010, the debt was calculated to be £8.494×10^{11}.

Use this information to estimate the national debt per person in the UK in February 2010.
Give your answer in standard form.

£ ....

[Total 2 marks]

---

9   The diagram below shows a trapezium. *FG* is parallel to *EH*.
EH is 15.5 cm, *EF* is 4.8 cm and *FG* is 10 cm.

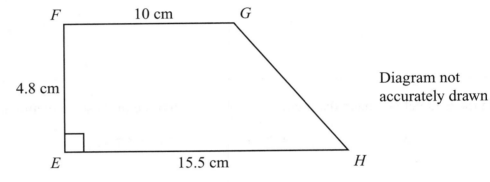

Diagram not accurately drawn

(a)   Calculate the length of *GH*.

.... cm
[3]

(b)   Calculate the size of angle *EHG*.
      Give your answer correct to 1 decimal place.

...................................°
[3]

[Total 6 marks]

Practice Paper 2

10 There are 128 students in Year 11. A teacher asks them all if they like football (F) and if they like badminton (B). He records the following results:

n(B) = 102
$F \cap B' = \emptyset$
n($F \cap B$) = 56

(a) Complete the Venn diagram below to show the number of elements.

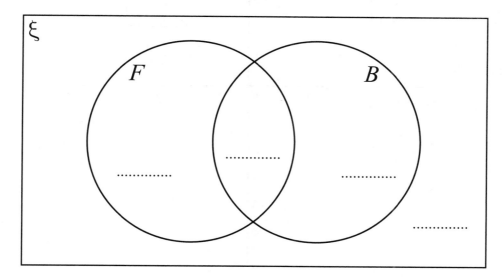

[2]

(b) Use the information in the Venn diagram to write a statement about students who like football in Year 11.

....

....

[1]

(c) Find n($F \cup B'$)

....

[1]

[Total 4 marks]

6

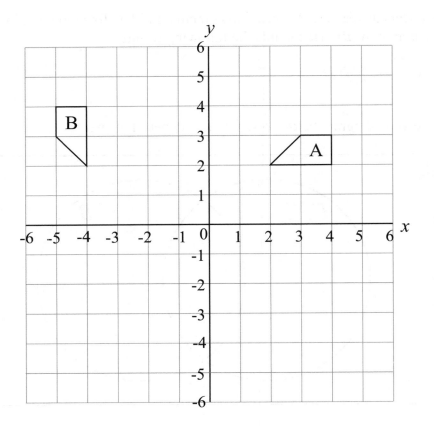

(a) Draw the reflection of shape A in the mirror line $y = -x$. Label this shape C.

[2]

(b) Describe the single transformation that maps shape A onto shape B.

[3]

[Total 5 marks]

12 Megan is the manager of a health club. She wants to know if the BMIs (Body Mass Indexes) of the female members have improved since she last surveyed them. She intends to publish her findings in an information leaflet. The cumulative frequency table below shows the new data she's collected from the 40 female members.

BMI (b)	Cumulative Frequency
$15 < b \leq 20$	4
$20 < b \leq 25$	18
$25 < b \leq 30$	30
$30 < b \leq 35$	35
$35 < b \leq 40$	38
$40 < b \leq 45$	40

(a) Use this information to draw a cumulative frequency graph on the axes below.

[2]

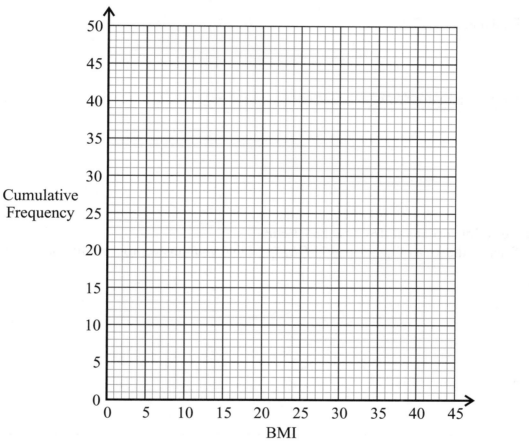

(b) Estimate the median BMI.

....

[1]

(c) Estimate the interquartile range (IQR).

....

[2]

[Total 5 marks]

8

Practice Paper 2

13   The quadrilaterals *ABCD* and *DEFG* are similar.

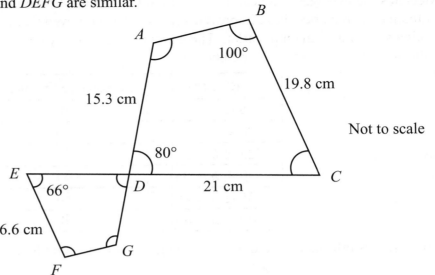

Not to scale

(a)   Find angle *DGF*.

........................°

[1]

(b)   Find the length of *ED*.

.... cm

[2]

The area of quadrilateral *ABCD* is 264.3 cm².

(c)   What is the area of quadrilateral *DEFG*? Give your answer to 3 significant figures.

.... cm²

[2]

[Total 5 marks]

9

Practice Paper 2

14 Heather is doing a blind taste-test for a jelly company. There are 3 pots of strawberry jelly, 2 pots of blackcurrant jelly, 1 pot of orange jelly and 2 pots of raspberry jelly. After a pot has been tasted, it is removed from the plate.

(a) Heather randomly selects one of the pots and tastes it. What is the probability that the pot contains either orange or strawberry jelly?

....
[2]

(b) Heather tests 2 jellies. What is the probability that she tries exactly **one** raspberry jelly?

....
[3]

[Total 5 marks]

15 The curve with equation $y = \frac{1}{3}x^3 - 3x^2 - 16x + 7$ has two turning points.

(a) Find $\frac{dy}{dx}$.

....
[2]

(b) Find the gradient when $x = 4$.

....
[1]

(c) Find the x-coordinates at the turning points of the curve.

....
[2]

[Total 5 marks]

Practice Paper 2

16 *ABCD* is a parallelogram.

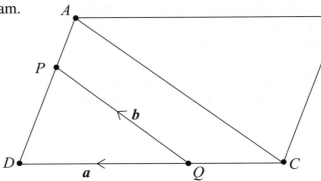

Diagram not
accurately drawn

$\overrightarrow{QP} = \boldsymbol{b}$ and $\overrightarrow{QD} = \boldsymbol{a}$.

Triangles *PQD* and *ACD* are similar.

$AD:PD = 5:3$

(a) Find $\overrightarrow{CA}$ in terms of $\boldsymbol{a}$ and $\boldsymbol{b}$.

....

[1]

R is a point on *AC* so that $5\overrightarrow{AR} = 2\overrightarrow{AC}$.

(b) Given that $\overrightarrow{PR} = k\overrightarrow{DQ}$, find the value of *k*.

$k = $ ....

[3]

[Total 4 marks]

---

17 A company is testing an air pressure gauge that is based on a gas-filled ball.

The air pressure is inversely proportional to the cube of the diameter of the ball.
When the air pressure, *p*, is 60 bars, the diameter of the ball, *d*, is 2 cm.

(a) Write down a formula connecting *p* and *d*.

....

[3]

(b) What diameter will the ball be when the pressure is 100 bars?
Give your answer correct to 2 decimal places.

.... cm

[2]

[Total 5 marks]

Practice Paper 2

18 Let $f(x) = 3x^2$ and $g(x) = \dfrac{3}{x-2}$

(a) Express the inverse function of $g(x)$ in the form $g^{-1}(x)$.

....

[2]

(b) Find the composite function $gf(x)$.

....

[2]

(c) Work out which values of x cannot be included in the domain of $gf(x)$.

$x = $ ....

[2]

[Total 6 marks]

19 A field contains 4 Herdwick sheep and 3 Texel sheep. One random sheep escapes from the field. Later on, another random sheep escapes.

(a) Complete the tree diagram.

[2]

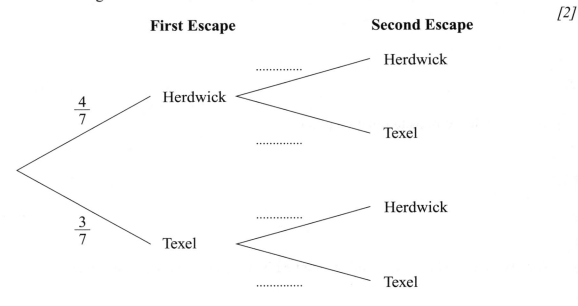

First Escape   **Second Escape**

$\frac{4}{7}$ Herdwick

.... Herdwick

.... Texel

$\frac{3}{7}$ Texel

.... Herdwick

.... Texel

(b) Find the probability that both escaped sheep are Herdwicks.

....

[2]

(c) Find the probability that a Herdwick and a Texel sheep escaped, in either order.

....

[2]

[Total 6 marks]

13

20 Solve $\dfrac{-54}{x+2} + \dfrac{11}{x} = 5$

....

[Total 5 marks]

21 Solve the simultaneous equations

$$y^2 + x^2 = 5$$
$$y = 2x + 4$$

....

[Total 6 marks]

[TOTAL FOR PAPER = 100 MARKS]

Answers

Section One — Numbers

Page 3: Prime Factors

1
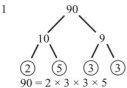
$90 = 2 \times 3 \times 3 \times 5$
[3 marks available — 2 marks for a correct method, 1 mark for all prime factors correct]

2 a) $2 \times 3 \times 5 \times 7$
[3 marks available — 2 marks for a correct method, 1 mark for all prime factors correct]

  b) $3 \times 3 \times 5 \times 5 \times 7 \times 7$
[3 marks available — 2 marks for a correct method, 1 mark for all prime factors correct]
"A correct method" here is either using a factor tree or just repeatedly dividing the factors until you get primes.

3 $25 \times 10^2 - 1 = 2499$, so $x = 10$ *[1 mark]*
Substituting 10 into factorised expression gives
$(5 \times 10 - 1)(5 \times 10 + 1) = 49 \times 51$ *[1 mark]*
$49 = 7^2$ and $51 = 17 \times 3$,
so 2499 as a product of its prime factors is $3 \times 7^2 \times 17$ *[1 mark]*
[3 marks available in total — as above]

Page 4: Common Multiples and Common Factors

1 a) $2 \times 2 \times 2 \times 3 \times 3$
[2 marks available — 1 mark for a correct method, 1 mark for all prime factors correct]

  b) Factors of 54 are: 1, 2, 3, 6, 9, (18), 27, 54
Factors of 72 are: 1, 2, 3, 4, 6, 8, 9, 12, (18), 24, 36, 72
So the HCF is 18 *[1 mark]*

  c) Multiples of 54 are: 54, 108, 162, (216), 270, ...
Multiples of 72 are: 72, 144, (216), 288, ...
So the LCM is 216 *[1 mark]*

2 Take out the common prime factors: $3 \times 5^2 = 75$.
[2 marks available — 1 mark for getting 3×5^2, 1 mark for correct answer]

3 Multiples of 6 are: 6, 12, 18, 24, 30, 36, 42, 48, 54, 60, 66, 72, 78, 84, 90, 96, 102, 108, 114, (120), 126, ...
Multiples of 8 are: 8, 16, 24, 32, 40, 48, 56, 64, 72, 80, 88, 96, 104, 112, (120), 128, ...
Multiples of 10 are: 10, 20, 30, 40, 50, 60, 70, 80, 90, 100, 110, (120), 130, ...

So the LCM is 120
[2 marks available — 1 mark for a correct method, 1 mark for LCM correct]

4 The first car takes 30 seconds to complete a circuit, the second car takes 70 seconds to complete a circuit.
Multiples of 30 are: 30, 60, 90, 120, 150, 180, (210), 240, ...
Multiples of 70 are: 70, 140, (210), 280, ...
So it will be 210 seconds or 3.5 minutes until they are side by side on the start line.
[2 marks available — 1 mark for a correct method, 1 mark for the correct answer]

Pages 5-6: Fractions

1 a) $\dfrac{4}{12} + \dfrac{3}{5} = \dfrac{20}{60} + \dfrac{36}{60} = \dfrac{56}{60} = \dfrac{14}{15}$
[2 marks available — 1 mark for writing over a common denominator, 1 mark for simplifying]

  b) $\dfrac{9}{10} - \dfrac{2}{8} = \dfrac{36}{40} - \dfrac{10}{40} = \dfrac{26}{40} = \dfrac{13}{20}$
[2 marks available — 1 mark for writing over a common denominator, 1 mark for simplifying]

2 a) $3\dfrac{1}{2} + 2\dfrac{3}{5} = \dfrac{7}{2} + \dfrac{13}{5} = \dfrac{35}{10} + \dfrac{26}{10} = \dfrac{35 + 26}{10} = \dfrac{61}{10}$ or $6\dfrac{1}{10}$
[3 marks available — 1 mark for writing as improper fractions, 1 mark for writing over a common denominator, 1 mark for the correct answer]

  b) $3\dfrac{3}{4} - 2\dfrac{1}{3} = \dfrac{15}{4} - \dfrac{7}{3} = \dfrac{45}{12} - \dfrac{28}{12} = \dfrac{45 - 28}{12} = \dfrac{17}{12}$ or $1\dfrac{5}{12}$
[3 marks available — 1 mark for writing as improper fractions, 1 mark for writing over a common denominator, 1 mark for the correct answer]
If you've used a different method in Q2, but still shown your working, and ended up with the same final answer, then you still get full marks.

3 $a = \dfrac{3}{4}, b = \dfrac{5}{2}$, so $\dfrac{1}{a} + \dfrac{1}{b} = \dfrac{4}{3} + \dfrac{2}{5} = \dfrac{20}{15} + \dfrac{6}{15} = \dfrac{26}{15}$ or $1\dfrac{11}{15}$
[3 marks available — 1 mark for reciprocal fractions, 1 mark for rewriting over a common denominator, 1 mark for the correct answer]

4 a) $1\dfrac{2}{3} \times \dfrac{9}{10} = \dfrac{5}{3} \times \dfrac{9}{10} = \dfrac{5 \times 9}{3 \times 10} = \dfrac{45}{30} = \dfrac{3}{2}$
[3 marks available — 1 mark for multiplying the two fractions together, 1 mark for an equivalent fraction, 1 mark for the correct final answer]

  b) $3\dfrac{1}{7} \times 1\dfrac{1}{7} = \dfrac{22}{7} \times \dfrac{8}{7} = \dfrac{22 \times 8}{7 \times 7}$ *[1 mark]*
$= \dfrac{176}{49}$ *[1 mark]*
[2 marks available in total — as above]

5 a) $\dfrac{3}{8} \div \dfrac{9}{10} = \dfrac{3}{8} \times \dfrac{10}{9} = \dfrac{3 \times 10}{8 \times 9} = \dfrac{30}{72} = \dfrac{5}{12}$
[2 marks available — 1 mark for taking the reciprocal and multiplying the two fractions together, 1 mark for the correct final answer]

  b) $3\dfrac{1}{2} \div 1\dfrac{3}{4} = \dfrac{7}{2} \div \dfrac{7}{4} = \dfrac{7}{2} \times \dfrac{4}{7} = \dfrac{7 \times 4}{2 \times 7} = \dfrac{28}{14} = 2$
[3 marks available — 1 mark for taking the reciprocal and multiplying the two fractions together, 1 mark for an equivalent fraction, 1 mark for the correct final answer]

6 a) $\dfrac{1}{3} + \dfrac{1}{6} + \dfrac{1}{4} = \dfrac{4}{12} + \dfrac{2}{12} + \dfrac{3}{12} = \dfrac{9}{12}$ *[1 mark]*
$1 - \dfrac{9}{12} = \dfrac{3}{12}$ *[1 mark]*
$= \dfrac{1}{4}$ *[1 mark]*
[3 marks available in total — as above]

  b) $\dfrac{1}{4} \times \dfrac{1}{2} = \dfrac{1}{8}$ of Lisa's dresses are blue and have sleeves. *[1 mark]*
The LCM of the denominators
of $\dfrac{1}{3}, \dfrac{1}{6}, \dfrac{1}{4}$, and $\dfrac{1}{8}$ is 24. *[1 mark]*
So Lisa has a minimum of 24 dresses in her wardrobe. *[1 mark]*
[3 marks available in total — as above]

Page 7: Fractions and Recurring Decimals

1 $10 \div 11 = 0.\dot{9}\dot{0}$ *[1 mark]*

2 $7 \div 33 = 0.\dot{2}\dot{1}$ *[1 mark]*

3 a) Let $r = 0.\dot{7}$, so $10r = 7.\dot{7}$
   $10r - r = 7.\dot{7} - 0.\dot{7}$
   $9r = 7$ *[1 mark]*
   $r = \frac{7}{9}$ *[1 mark]*
   [2 marks available in total — as above]

   b) Let $r = 0.\dot{2}\dot{6}$, so $100r = 26.\dot{2}\dot{6}$
   $100r - r = 26.\dot{2}\dot{6} - 0.\dot{2}\dot{6}$
   $99r = 26$ *[1 mark]*
   $r = \frac{26}{99}$ *[1 mark]*
   [2 marks available in total — as above]

   c) Let $r = 1.\dot{3}\dot{6}$, so $100r = 136.\dot{3}\dot{6}$
   $100r - r = 136.\dot{3}\dot{6} - 1.\dot{3}\dot{6}$
   $99r = 135$ *[1 mark]*
   $r = \frac{135}{99}$
   $r = \frac{15}{11}$ or $1\frac{4}{11}$ *[1 mark]*
   [2 marks available in total — as above]

4 Let $10r = 5.\dot{9}\dot{0}$, so $1000r = 590.\dot{9}\dot{0}$
   $990r = 585$ *[1 mark]*
   $r = \frac{585}{990} = \frac{13}{22}$ *[1 mark]*
   [2 marks available in total — as above]

Pages 8-9: Percentages

1 Number of male micro pigs $= 40 - 24 = 16$ *[1 mark]*
   Fraction male $= \frac{16}{40} = \frac{2}{5}$ *[1 mark]*
   So percentage male $= 40\%$ *[1 mark]*
   [3 marks available in total — as above]

2 a) $20\% = 20 \div 100 = 0.2$
   $0.2 \times £395 = £79$ *[1 mark]*
   $£395 + £79$ *[1 mark]*
   $= £474$ *[1 mark]*
   [3 marks available in total — as above]
   You could work out the multiplier (1 + 0.2 = 1.2) then multiply by the cost to find the total price £395 × 1.2 = £474.

   b) $1\% = 99 \div 20 = £4.95$ *[1 mark]*
   $100\% = 4.95 \times 100 = £495$ *[1 mark]*
   Total $= 495 + 99 = £594$ *[1 mark]*
   [3 marks available in total — as above]

3 $£15\,714 = 108\%$
   $£15\,714 \div 108 = £145.50 = 1\%$ *[1 mark]*
   $£145.50 \times 100 = 100\%$ *[1 mark]*
   $= £14\,550$ *[1 mark]*
   [3 marks available in total — as above]

4 a) $36 - 30 = 6$ *[1 mark]*
   $\frac{6}{30} \times 100$ *[1 mark]*
   $= 20\%$ *[1 mark]*
   [3 marks available in total — as above]

   b) 135 cm $= 112.5\%$
   135 cm $\div 112.5 = 1.2$ cm $= 1\%$ *[1 mark]*
   1.2 cm $\times 100$ *[1 mark]*
   $= 120$ cm $= 100\%$ *[1 mark]*
   [3 marks available in total — as above]

5 a) $18\,500 - 12\,600 = £5900$ *[1 mark]*
   $\frac{5900}{18\,500} \times 100$ *[1 mark]*
   $= 31.891... = 31.9\%$ *[1 mark]*
   [3 marks available in total — as above]

   b) $\frac{11\,549}{70}$ *[1 mark]*
   $= 164.9857...$
   $164.9857... \times 100$ *[1 mark]*
   $= £16\,498.57... = £16\,499$ *[1 mark]*
   [3 marks available in total — as above]

6 $1.25 \times 1.16 = 1.45$
   So the prize money increased by 45% between 1974 and 2014.
   [3 marks available in total — 1 mark for at least one of 1.25 and 1.16, 1 mark for a correct calculation and 1 mark for correct final answer of 45%]

Page 10: Compound Growth and Depreciation

1 Population after 15 years $= 2000 \times \left(1 - \frac{8}{100}\right)^{15}$
   $= 2000 \times (0.92)^{15}$
   $= 572.59... = 573$ fish.
   [3 marks available — 1 mark for a correct formula, 1 mark for substituting numbers correctly and 1 mark for correct answer]

2 $£120\,000 \times \left(1 + \frac{15}{100}\right)^{5} = £241\,362.86... = £241\,000$ (to nearest 1000)
   [3 marks available — 1 mark for a correct formula, 1 mark for substituting numbers correctly and 1 mark for correct answer]

3 $£3995 \div \left(1 - \frac{11}{100}\right)^{6} = £8038.53... = £8000$ (to nearest £100)
   [3 marks available — 1 mark for a correct formula, 1 mark for substituting numbers correctly and 1 mark for correct answer]

4 Let r be the interest rate.
   $£2704 = £2500 \times \left(1 + \frac{r}{100}\right)^{2}$ *[1 mark]*
   $\frac{£2704}{£2500} = \left(1 + \frac{r}{100}\right)^{2}$
   $1 + \frac{r}{100} = \sqrt{\frac{£2704}{£2500}} = 1.04$ *[1 mark]*
   interest rate $= 4\%$ *[1 mark]*
   [3 marks available in total — as above]

Pages 11-12: Ratios and Proportion

1 $5 + 6 + 6 + 7 = 24$ *[1 mark]*
   $96 \div 24 = 4$ *[1 mark]*
   $4 \times 7 = 28$ cm *[1 mark]*
   [3 marks available in total — as above]

2 a) $15 : 6 = 5 : 2$ *[1 mark]*

   b) 1355 ml $\div 5 = 271$ ml *[1 mark]*
   271 ml $\times 2 = 542$ ml *[1 mark]*
   [2 marks available in total — as above]
   If your answer to part a) was incorrect, but your answer to part b) was correct for your incorrect ratio, you still get the marks for part b).

3 $286 \div 13 = 22$ *[1 mark]*
   $22 \times (5 + 1)$ *[1 mark]*
   $= 132$ in total *[1 mark]*
   [3 marks available in total — as above]

4 Real-life length of the bridge: $133 \times 38 = 5054$ cm *[1 mark]*
   Ashim's scale is $53.2 : 5054$,
   $5054 \div 53.2 = 95$
   So Ashim is using a scale of $1 : 95$. *[1 mark]*
   [2 marks available in total — as above]

5 $\frac{1}{3}$ of £21\,000 $= \frac{1}{3} \times £21\,000 = £21\,000 \div 3$
   $= £7000$ on staff training & new exhibits *[1 mark]*
   $£7000 \div (2 + 5) = £7000 \div 7 = £1000$ *[1 mark]*
   $£1000 \times 5 = £5000$ on new exhibits *[1 mark]*
   [3 marks available in total — as above]

6 Cost of 1 glass slipper $= £86.25 \div 23 = £3.75$ *[1 mark]*
   Cost of 35 glass slippers $= £3.75 \times 35 = £131.25$ *[1 mark]*
   [2 marks available in total — as above]

7 a) $\frac{18}{12} = \frac{3}{2}$ *[1 mark]*
   $\frac{3}{2} \times 150$ g $= 225$ g *[1 mark]*
   [2 marks available in total — as above]

   b) $300 \div 75 = 4$ *[1 mark]*
   4×12 flapjacks $= 48$ flapjacks *[1 mark]*
   [2 marks available in total — as above]

Page 13: Rounding Numbers and Estimating

1 a) $\dfrac{197.8}{\sqrt{0.01 + 0.23}} = \dfrac{197.8}{\sqrt{0.24}} = \dfrac{197.8}{0.489897948...} = 403.757559...$

[2 marks available — 1 mark for some correct working, 1 mark for answer correct to 4 decimal places]

   b) 404 *[1 mark]*

   In questions 1 and 2, if you get part a) wrong but round your wrong answer correctly in part b) you'll still get the mark for part b).

2 a) $\sqrt{\dfrac{12.71 + 137.936}{\cos 50° \times 13.2^2}} = \sqrt{\dfrac{150.646}{0.642787609... \times 174.24}}$

$= \sqrt{1.34506182...}$

$= 1.1597680...$

[2 marks available — 1 mark for some correct working, 1 mark for answer correct to 4 decimal places]

   b) 1.16 *[1 mark]*

3 a) $\dfrac{215.7 \times 44.8}{460} \approx \dfrac{200 \times 40}{500} = \dfrac{8000}{500} = 16$

[3 marks available — 1 mark for correctly rounding 1 number to 1 significant figure, 1 mark for correctly rounding the other 2 numbers to 1 significant figure, 1 mark for correct answer]

   b) The answer to a) will be smaller than the exact answer, because in the rounded fraction the numerator is smaller and denominator is larger compared to the exact calculation.
   [2 marks available — 1 mark for 'smaller than the exact answer', 1 mark for correct reasoning]

Pages 14-15: Bounds

1 a) Upper bound = 62.5 cm *[1 mark]*
   b) Lower bound = 61.5 cm *[1 mark]*

2 Upper bound of x = 2.25 *[1 mark]*
   So upper bound of $4x + 3 = 4 \times 2.25 + 3 = 12$ *[1 mark]*
   Lower bound of x = 2.15 *[1 mark]*
   So lower bound of $4x + 3 = 4 \times 2.15 + 3 = 11.6$ *[1 mark]*
   [4 marks available in total — as above]

3 a) 54.05 cm *[1 mark]*
   b) Lower bound for the width of the paper = 23.55 cm *[1 mark]*
      Lower bound for the perimeter = (54.05 cm × 2) + (23.55 cm × 2)
      = 155.2 cm *[1 mark]*
      [2 marks available in total — as above]

4 Upper bound for x = 57.5 mm *[1 mark]*
   Upper bound for y = 32.5 mm *[1 mark]*
   Upper bound for area = 57.5 mm × 32.5 mm = 1868.75 mm²
   = 1870 mm² to 3 s.f. *[1 mark]*
   [3 marks available in total — as above]

5 Lower bound of difference = 13.65 − 8.35 *[1 mark]*
   = 5.3 litres *[1 mark]*
   [2 marks available in total — as above]

6 Upper bound of area = 5.25 cm² *[1 mark]*
   Lower bound of height = 3.15 cm *[1 mark]*
   2 × (5.25 ÷ 3.15) = 3.33 to 2 d.p. *[1 mark]*
   [3 marks available — as above]

7 Lower bound for distance = 99.5 m
   Upper bound for time = 12.55 s *[1 mark for both]*

   Lower bound for speed $= \dfrac{99.5}{12.55}$ m/s

   = 7.928... m/s *[1 mark]*
   Lower bound for speed to 2 s.f. = 7.9 m/s
   Lower bound for speed to 1 s.f. = 8 m/s

   Upper bound for distance = 100.5 m
   Lower bound for time = 12.45 s *[1 mark for both]*

   Upper bound for speed $= \dfrac{100.5}{12.45}$ m/s

   = 8.072... m/s *[1 mark]*
   Upper bound for speed to 2 s.f. = 8.1 m/s
   Upper bound for speed to 1 s.f. = 8 m/s

   The lower bound to 2 s.f. does not equal the upper bound to 2 s.f., but the lower bound to 1 s.f. does equal the upper bound to 1 s.f. So Dan's speed is 8 m/s to 1 significant figure.
   [1 mark for comparing bounds to reach correct answer to 1 s.f.]
   [5 marks available in total — as above]

Page 16: Standard Form

1 a) $A = 4.834 \times 10^9 = 4\ 834\ 000\ 000$ *[1 mark]*
   b) $C = 5.81 \times 10^{-3} = 0.00581$ *[1 mark]*
   c) C, B, A $(5.81 \times 10^{-3}, 2.7 \times 10^5, 4.834 \times 10^9)$ *[1 mark]*

2 $(4.5 \times 10^9) \div (1.5 \times 10^8) = 30$ *[1 mark]*
   1 : 30 *[1 mark]*
   [2 marks available in total — as above]

3 a) $2.1 \times 10^5 = 0.021 \times 10^7$ *[1 mark]*
      $7.59 \times 10^7 + 0.021 \times 10^7 = 7.611 \times 10^7$ kg *[1 mark]*
      [2 marks available in total — as above]
   b) $(2.1 \times 10^5) \div (7.611 \times 10^7) = 0.002759...$ *[1 mark]*
      $0.002759 \times 100 = 0.28$ % (to 2 d.p.) *[1 mark]*
      [2 marks available in total — as above]

Page 17: Sets

1 a) 3, 6, 8, 9, 12, 14, 15 *[1 mark]*
   b) 6, 12 *[1 mark]*

2 a) There are 5 students who are in both the cycling and football clubs. *[1 mark]*
   b) There are no students who are in both the basketball and football clubs. *[1 mark]*

3 3, 9, 15
   [2 marks available — 2 marks for correct answer, otherwise 1 mark for 1 or more members correct]

Pages 18-19: Venn Diagrams

1
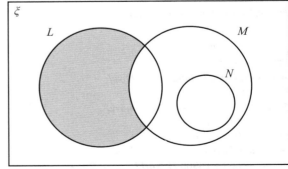

[2 marks available — 1 mark for correct shaded area, 1 mark for correct N]

2 a)

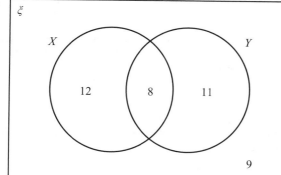

[2 marks available — 2 marks for all numbers correct, otherwise 1 mark for 2 or 3 numbers correct]

b) 11 *[1 mark]*

c) 9 *[1 mark]*

3 E.g.

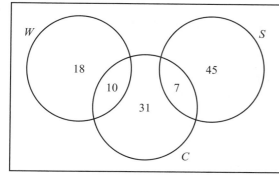

18 + 10 + 31 + 7 + 45 = 111 customers

[3 marks available — 2 marks for complete, correct Venn diagram, 1 mark for correct total number of customers]

If you answered this question a different way, but got the correct number of customers, and showed how you worked it out, then give yourself full marks.

a) 8 + 5 + 4 + 2 + 7 + 3 = 29 *[1 mark]*

b) 5 + 6 = 11 *[1 mark]*

c) 2 *[1 mark]*

d) 6 + 3 + 7 + 1 + 5 + 2 + 4 = 28 *[1 mark]*

Section Two — Algebra

Pages 20-21: Powers and Roots

a) $a \times a \times a \times a \times a \times a \times a = a^7$ *[1 mark]*

b) $x^7 \div x = x^{7-1} = x^6$ *[1 mark]*

c) $(d^9)^2 = d^{9 \times 2} = d^{18}$ *[1 mark]*

so $\dfrac{(d^9)^2}{d^4} = \dfrac{d^{18}}{d^4} = d^{18-4} = d^{14}$ *[1 mark]*

[2 marks available in total — as above]

a) $3^0 = 1$ *[1 mark]*

b) $5^{-2} = \dfrac{1}{5^2} = \dfrac{1}{25}$ or 0.04 *[1 mark]*

c) $8^{\frac{4}{3}} = (8^{\frac{1}{3}})^4 = (2)^4 = 16$

[2 marks available — 1 mark for correct working, 1 mark for the correct final answer]

a) $2 \times 4 \times 8 = 2 \times 2^2 \times 2^3$ *[1 mark]*

$= 2^{1+2+3} = 2^6$ *[1 mark]*

[2 marks available in total — as above]

b) $\dfrac{(2 \times 2 \times 16)^2}{8} = \dfrac{(2^1 \times 2^1 \times 2^4)^2}{2^3}$ *[1 mark]*

$= \dfrac{(2^{1+1+4})^2}{2^3} = \dfrac{(2^6)^2}{2^3} = \dfrac{2^{6 \times 2}}{2^3} = \dfrac{2^{12}}{2^3}$ *[1 mark]*

$= 2^{12-3} = 2^9$ *[1 mark]*

[3 marks available in total — as above]

The questions says 'without a calculator' so you won't get full marks unless you show some working.

4 a) $4a \times 6b = 24ab$ *[1 mark]*

b) $3a^3 \times 2ab^2 = (3 \times 2) \times (a^3 \times a) \times b^2 = 6a^4b^2$

[2 marks available — 1 mark for correct working, 1 mark for the correct answer]

c) $\dfrac{4a^5b^3}{2ab^2} = (4 \div 2) \times (a^5 \div a) \times (b^3 \div b^2) = 2a^4b$

[2 marks available — 1 mark for correct working, 1 mark for the correct answer]

5 a) $\dfrac{1}{100} = \dfrac{1}{10^2} = 10^{-2}$, so $k = -2$ *[1 mark]*

b) $(\sqrt{9})^8 = (9^{\frac{1}{2}})^8$ *[1 mark]*

$= 9^{\frac{1}{2} \times 8} = 9^4$ so $k = 4$ *[1 mark]*

[2 marks available in total — as above]

c) $(3^4)^2 = 3^{4 \times 2} = 3^8$ and $\dfrac{3^5}{3^{11}} = 3^{5-11} = 3^{-6}$ *[1 mark]*

so $(3^4)^2 \times \dfrac{3^5}{3^{11}} = 3^8 \times 3^{-6} = 3^2$ and $k = 2$ *[1 mark]*

[2 marks available in total — as above]

6 $(9a^4)^{\frac{1}{2}} = \sqrt{9a^4} = 3a^2$ *[1 mark]*

$\dfrac{2ab^2}{6a^3b} = \dfrac{2}{6} \times \dfrac{a}{a^3} \times \dfrac{b^2}{b} = \dfrac{1}{3} \times \dfrac{1}{a^2} \times b = \dfrac{b}{3a^2}$ *[1 mark]*

so $(9a^4)^{\frac{1}{2}} \times \dfrac{2ab^2}{6a^3b} = 3a^2 \times \dfrac{b}{3a^2} = b$ *[1 mark]*

[3 marks available in total — as above]

Page 22: Making Formulas from Words

1 a) $A = 3x \times 3x$

$A = 9x^2$ *[1 mark]*

b) $A = 9 \times 4^2 = 144 \text{ cm}^2$ *[1 mark]*

2 a) $C = 10p + e$

[2 marks available — 2 marks for the correct expression, otherwise 1 mark for the correct coefficient on the p variable]

b) $e = 8 \times 4 = 32$ *[1 mark]*

$C = (10 \times 4) + 32 = 72$ so total cost = £72 *[1 mark]*

[2 marks available in total — as above]

3 a) The amount that Peter paid is given by $\dfrac{T}{2}$.

The amount that Marek paid is $3 + 0.5d$.

If they paid the same amount, then $3 + 0.5d = \dfrac{T}{2}$. *[1 mark]*

b) $\dfrac{T}{2} = 3 + 0.5d$, so $T = 6 + d$ *[1 mark]*

When $d = 2$, $T = 6 + 2 = 8$, so cost = £8 *[1 mark]*

[2 marks available in total — as above]

Page 23: Multiplying Out Brackets

1 a) $3(x - 1) = (3 \times x) + (3 \times -1) = 3x - 3$ *[1 mark]*

b) $4a(a + 2b) = (4a \times a) + (4a \times 2b) = 4a^2 + 8ab$ *[1 mark]*

c) $8p^2(3 - 2p) - 2p(p - 3)$

$= [(8p^2 \times 3) + (8p^2 \times -2p)] - [(2p \times p) + (2p \times -3)]$

$= 24p^2 - 16p^3 - 2p^2 + 6p$ *[1 mark]*

$= 22p^2 - 16p^3 + 6p$ *[1 mark]*

[2 marks available in total — as above]

2 a) $(2t - 5)(3t + 4) = (2t \times 3t) + (2t \times 4) + (-5 \times 3t) + (-5 \times 4)$

$= 6t^2 + 8t - 15t - 20$

$= 6t^2 - 7t - 20$ *[1 mark]*

[2 marks available in total — as above]

b) $(x + 3)^2 = (x + 3)(x + 3)$

$= (x \times x) + (x \times 3) + (3 \times x) + (3 \times 3)$

$= x^2 + 3x + 3x + 9$ *[1 mark]*

$= x^2 + 6x + 9$ *[1 mark]*

[2 marks available in total — as above]

3 $a = 4(3b - 1) + 6(5 - 2b)$

$a = (4 \times 3b) + (4 \times -1) + (6 \times 5) + (6 \times -2b)$

$a = 12b - 4 + 30 - 12b$

$a = 26$

[2 marks available — 1 mark for correctly expanding the brackets, 1 mark for simplifying to a = 26]

4   Area = ½ × base × height
    = ½ × (3x + 5) × (2x − 4) = ½ (3x + 5)(2x − 4)   *[1 mark]*
    = ½ × [(3x × 2x) + (3x × −4) + (5 × 2x) + (5 × −4)]
    = ½ × (6x² − 12x + 10x − 20)
    = ½ × (6x² − 2x − 20)   *[1 mark]*
    = 3x² − x − 10   *[1 mark]*
    [3 marks available in total — as above]
    You could also have multiplied (2x − 4) by ½ first of all. The area would then just be (3x + 5)(x −2), which is a bit simpler to multiply out.

Page 24: Factorising

1   4a² − 24ab = 4(a² − 6ab)   *[1 mark]*
    = 4a(a − 6b)   *[1 mark]*
    [2 marks available in total — as above]

2   a)   6x + 3 = 3(2x + 1)   *[1 mark]*
    b)   7y − 21y² = 7(y − 3y²)   *[1 mark]*
    = 7y(1 − 3y)   *[1 mark]*
    [2 marks available in total — as above]
    c)   2v³w + 8v²w² = 2(v³w + 4v²w²)   *[1 mark]*
    = 2v²w(v + 4w)   *[1 mark]*
    [2 marks available in total — as above]

3   a)   x² − 16 = x² − 4² = (x + 4)(x − 4)
    [2 marks available — 2 marks for the correct answer, allow 1 mark for (x + 4)² or (x − 4)²]
    b)   9n² − 4m² = (3n)² − (2m)²   *[1 mark]*
    = (3n + 2m)(3n − 2m)   *[1 mark]*
    [2 marks available in total — as above]

Page 25: Manipulating Surds

1   (2 + √3)(5 − √3) = (2 × 5) + (2 × −√3) + (√3 × 5) + (√3 × −√3)
    = 10 − 2√3 + 5√3 − 3
    = 7 + 3√3
    [2 marks available — 1 mark for correct working, 1 mark for the correct answer]

2   √45 = √9 √5 = 3√5   *[1 mark]*
    So 3√5 + a√5 = 10√5   *[1 mark]*
    3 + a = 10
    a = 7   *[1 mark]*
    [3 marks available in total — as above]

3   √27 = √9 × √3 = 3√3
    So $\frac{(\sqrt{27} + 6)}{\sqrt{3}} = \frac{(3\sqrt{3} + 6)}{\sqrt{3}} = \frac{\sqrt{3}(3\sqrt{3} + 6)}{3} = \frac{9 + 6\sqrt{3}}{3}$
    = 3 + 2√3, so a = 3 and b = 2.
    [3 marks available — 1 mark for correctly simplifying √27, 1 mark for rationalising the denominator, 1 mark for the correct answer]

4   (√3 + a√5)² = √3 √3 + a√3 √5 + a√3 √5 + a² √5 √5   *[1 mark]*
    = 3 + a√15 + a√15 + 5a²
    = (3 + 5a²) + 2a√15   *[1 mark]*
    (3 + 5a²) + 2a√15 = b + 4√15
    2a√15 = 4√15
    a = 2
    b = 3 + 5a² = 3 + (5 × 2²) = 23   *[1 mark for both a and b]*
    [3 marks available in total — as above]

Pages 26-27: Solving Equations

1   a)   40 − 3x = 17x,   40 = 17x + 3x,   40 = 20x,   x = $\frac{40}{20}$ = 2
    [2 marks available — 1 mark for adding 3x to both sides, 1 mark for the correct answer]
    b)   2y − 5 = 3y − 12,   12 − 5 = 3y − 2y,   y = 7
    [3 marks available — 1 mark for rearrangement with y terms on one side and numbers on the other, 1 mark for collecting like terms on at least one side, 1 mark for the correct answer]

c)   2r − 6 = 3(3 − r),   2r − 6 = 9 − 3r,   2r + 3r = 9 + 6,   5r = 15,
    r = $\frac{15}{5}$ = 3
    [3 marks available — 1 mark for expanding out the bracket, 1 mark for adding 6 and 3r to both sides, 1 mark for the correct answer]

2   a)   9b − 7 = 2(3b + 1),   9b − 7 = 6b + 2,   9b − 6b = 2 + 7,   3b = 9
    b = $\frac{9}{3}$ = 3
    [3 marks available — 1 mark for expanding out the bracket, 1 mark for adding 7 and subtracting 6b from each side, 1 mark for the correct answer]
    b) $\frac{28 − z}{4}$ = 5,   28 − z = 20,   z = 28 − 20,   z = 8
    [2 marks available — 1 mark for multiplying both sides by 4, 1 mark for correct answer]

3   $\frac{8 − 2x}{3} + \frac{2x + 4}{9}$ = 12
    $\frac{9(8 − 2x)}{3} + \frac{9(2x + 4)}{9}$ = 108
    3(8 − 2x) + (2x + 4) = 108   *[1 mark]*
    24 − 6x + 2x + 4 = 108
    6x − 2x = 24 + 4 − 108   *[1 mark]*
    4x = −80   *[1 mark]*
    x = −20   *[1 mark]*
    [4 marks available in total — as above]

4   The perimeter is (2x − 2) + (x + 1) + (22 − x) + (3x + 2), so...
    (2x − 2) + (x + 1) + (22 − x) + (3x + 2) = 58   *[1 mark]*
    2x + x − x + 3x = 58 + 2 − 1 − 22 − 2   *[1 mark]*
    5x = 35
    x = 7   *[1 mark]*
    [3 marks available in total — as above]

5   a)   2(5x − 8) + 2(2x + 3) = 2(3x + 6) + 2y   *[1 mark]*
    14x − 10 = 6x + 12 + 2y   *[1 mark]*
    8x − 22 = 2y
    y = 4x − 11   *[1 mark]*
    [3 marks available in total — as above]
    b)   14x − 10 = 32   *[1 mark]*
    14x = 42
    x = 3   *[1 mark]*
    y = 4x − 11 so if x = 3, y = 1   *[1 mark]*
    [3 marks available in total — as above]

Pages 28-29: Formulas

1   a)   y = $\frac{x − 2}{3}$, so 3y = x − 2 and x = 3y + 2
    [2 marks available — 1 mark for multiplying both sides by 3, 1 mark for the correct answer]
    b)   When y = 5, x = (3 × 5) + 2 = 15 + 2 = 17
    [2 marks available — 1 mark for correct substitution, 1 mark for the correct answer]

2   a)   V = $\frac{1}{3}$Ah, so 3V = Ah and h = $\frac{3V}{A}$
    [2 marks available — 1 mark for multiplying both sides by 3, 1 mark for the correct answer]
    b)   When V = 18 and A = 12, h = $\frac{3 × 18}{12} = \frac{54}{12}$ = 4.5 cm
    [2 marks available — 1 mark for correct substitution, 1 mark for the correct answer]

3   a)   s = $\frac{1}{2}$ × −9.8 × 8²   *[1 mark]*
    = −313.6   *[1 mark]*
    [2 marks available in total — as above]
    b)   s = $\frac{1}{2}$gt², so gt² = 2s,
    t² = $\frac{2s}{g}$ *[1 mark]*,
    t = $\sqrt{\frac{2s}{g}}$ *[1 mark]*
    [2 marks available in total — as above]

4 a) $a + y = \dfrac{b - y}{a}$, so...

$a(a + y) = b - y$ *[1 mark]*, $a^2 + ay = b - y$,

$ay + y = b - a^2$ *[1 mark]*, $y(a + 1) = b - a^2$ *[1 mark]*,

$y = \dfrac{b - a^2}{a + 1}$ *[1 mark]*

[4 marks available in total — as above]

b) When $a = 3$ and $b = 6$, $y = \dfrac{6 - 3^2}{3 + 1} = -\dfrac{3}{4}$ or -0.75

[2 marks available — 1 mark for correct substitution, 1 mark for the correct answer]

5 $x = \sqrt{\dfrac{(1 + n)}{(1 - n)}}$, so $x^2 = \dfrac{(1 + n)}{(1 - n)}$ *[1 mark]*, $x^2(1 - n) = 1 + n$,

$x^2 - x^2 n = 1 + n$ *[1 mark]*, $x^2 - 1 = n + x^2 n$ *[1 mark]*,

$x^2 - 1 = n(1 + x^2)$ *[1 mark]*,

$n = \dfrac{x^2 - 1}{1 + x^2}$ *[1 mark]*

[5 marks available in total — as above]

6 $\dfrac{p(x + 4)}{5x(x + 4)} + \dfrac{5px^2}{5x(x + 4)} = \dfrac{2(5x)(x + 4)}{5x(x + 4)}$ *[1 mark]*

$p(x + 4) + 5px^2 = 2(5x)(x + 4)$ *[1 mark]*

$p(5x^2 + x + 4) = 2(5x)(x + 4)$ *[1 mark]*

$p = \dfrac{2(5x)(x + 4)}{5x^2 + x + 4}$ *[1 mark]*

$p = \dfrac{10x^2 + 40x}{5x^2 + x + 4}$ *[1 mark]*

[5 marks available in total — as above]

Page 30: Factorising Quadratics

1 a) $(x - 4)(x + 8)$

[2 marks available — 1 mark for correct numbers in brackets, 1 mark for correct signs]

b) $(3x + 2)(x - 2)$

[2 marks available — 1 mark for correct numbers in brackets, 1 mark for correct signs]

2 a) $(5x - 9)(x - 2)$

[2 marks available — 1 mark for correct numbers in brackets, 1 mark for correct signs]

b) $(5x - 9)(x - 2) = (x - 2)^2$ *[1 mark]*

$(5x - 9)(x - 2) - (x - 2)^2 = 0$

$(x - 2)((5x - 9) - (x - 2)) = 0$ *[1 mark]*

$x - 2 = 0$ or $5x - 9 - x + 2 = 0$ *[1 mark]*

$x = 2$ or $4x - 7 = 0$

$4x = 7$

$x = \dfrac{7}{4} = 1.75$

[1 mark for both solutions]

[4 marks available in total — as above]

3 a) The area of the square is $(x + 3)(x + 3) = x^2 + 6x + 9$. *[1 mark]*

The area of the triangle is $\frac{1}{2}(2x + 2)(x + 3)$

$= \frac{1}{2}(2x^2 + 6x + 2x + 6) = \frac{1}{2}(2x^2 + 8x + 6)$

$= x^2 + 4x + 3$ *[1 mark]*

So the area of the whole shape is $x^2 + 6x + 9 + x^2 + 4x + 3$

$= 2x^2 + 10x + 12$ *[1 mark]*

$2x^2 + 10x + 12 = 60$, so $2x^2 + 10x - 48 = 0$ *[1 mark]*

[4 marks available in total — as above]

b) $2x^2 + 10x - 48 = 0$

$(2x - 6)(x + 8) = 0$ *[1 mark]*

$2x - 6 = 0$ or $x + 8 = 0$

$x = 3$ or $x = -8$

[1 mark for both solutions]

A length can't have a negative value so the answer must be $x = 3$ *[1 mark]*

[3 marks available in total — as above]

Page 31: The Quadratic Formula

1 $a = 1$, $b = 5$ and $c = 3$

$x = \dfrac{-5 \pm \sqrt{5^2 - 4 \times 1 \times 3}}{2 \times 1} = \dfrac{-5 \pm \sqrt{13}}{2}$

$x = -0.70$ or $x = -4.30$

[3 marks available — 1 mark for correct substitution, 1 mark for each correct solution]

2 $a = 1$, $b = 6$ and $c = -3$

$x = \dfrac{-6 \pm \sqrt{6^2 - 4 \times 1 \times -3}}{2 \times 1} = \dfrac{-6 \pm \sqrt{48}}{2}$

$x = 0.46$ or $x = -6.46$

[3 marks available — 1 mark for correct substitution, 1 mark for each correct solution]

3 $a = 2$, $b = -7$ and $c = 2$

$x = \dfrac{-(-7) \pm \sqrt{(-7)^2 - 4 \times 2 \times 2}}{2 \times 2} = \dfrac{7 \pm \sqrt{33}}{4}$

$x = 3.19$ or $x = 0.31$

[3 marks available — 1 mark for correct substitution, 1 mark for each correct solution]

4 $a = 3$, $b = -2$ and $c = -4$

$x = \dfrac{-(-2) \pm \sqrt{(-2)^2 - 4 \times 3 \times -4}}{2 \times 3} = \dfrac{2 \pm \sqrt{52}}{6}$

$x = \dfrac{1 + \sqrt{13}}{3}$ or $x = \dfrac{1 - \sqrt{13}}{3}$

[3 marks available — 1 mark for correct substitution, 1 mark for each correct solution]

Page 32: Algebraic Fractions

1 a) $\dfrac{3x - 12}{x^2 - 16} = \dfrac{3(x - 4)}{(x + 4)(x - 4)} = \dfrac{3}{x + 4}$

[3 marks available — 1 mark for correctly factorising the denominator, 1 mark for correctly factorising the numerator, 1 mark for the correct answer]

b) $\dfrac{x^2 - 4}{x^2 + 8x + 12} = \dfrac{(x + 2)(x - 2)}{(x + 2)(x + 6)} = \dfrac{x - 2}{x + 6}$

[3 marks available — 1 mark for correctly factorising the denominator, 1 mark for correctly factorising the numerator, 1 mark for the correct answer]

2 a) $\dfrac{x^2}{3x} \times \dfrac{6}{x + 1} = \dfrac{6x^2}{3x(x + 1)} = \dfrac{2x}{x + 1}$

[2 marks available — 1 mark for correct multiplication, 1 mark for the correct answer]

b) $\dfrac{10x}{3 + x} \div \dfrac{4}{5(3 + x)} = \dfrac{10x}{3 + x} \times \dfrac{5(3 + x)}{4} = \dfrac{50x(3 + x)}{4(3 + x)} = \dfrac{50x}{4} = \dfrac{25x}{2}$

[3 marks available — 1 mark for converting to a multiplication, 1 mark for correct multiplication, 1 mark for correct answer]

3 $\dfrac{3(4x - 3)}{(2x + 1)(4x - 3)} = \dfrac{7(2x + 1)}{(2x + 1)(4x - 3)}$

$3(4x - 3) = 7(2x + 1)$ *[1 mark]*

$12x - 9 = 14x + 7$ *[1 mark]*

$-16 = 2x$ *[1 mark]*

$x = -8$ *[1 mark]*

[4 marks available in total — as above]

4 $\dfrac{12x}{x(x + 4)} + \dfrac{2(x + 4)}{x(x + 4)} = \dfrac{3x(x + 4)}{x(x + 4)}$ *[1 mark]*

$12x + 2(x + 4) = 3x(x + 4)$

$12x + 2x + 8 = 3x^2 + 12x$ *[1 mark]*

$3x^2 - 2x - 8 = 0$ *[1 mark]*

$(3x + 4)(x - 2) = 0$ *[1 mark]*

$x = -\dfrac{4}{3}$ or $x = 2$ *[1 mark for both solutions]*

[5 marks available in total — as above]

Page 33: Inequalities

1 $-3, -2, -1, 0, 1$
   *[2 marks available — 2 marks for all five numbers correct,
   otherwise 1 mark for four correct numbers]*

2 $9 < 2p \leq 18$, so $4.5 < p \leq 9$ *[1 mark]*
   $p = 5, 6, 7, 8$ or 9 *[2 marks for all five numbers correct,
   otherwise 1 mark for four correct numbers]*
   [3 marks available in total — as above]

3 a) $4q - 5 < 23$, so $4q < 28$ *[1 mark]* and $q < 7$ *[1 mark]*
      [2 marks available in total — as above]

   b) $\frac{2x}{5} \leq 3$, so $2x \leq 15$ *[1 mark]* and $x \leq 7.5$ *[1 mark]*
      [2 marks available in total — as above]

   c) $x^2 + 1 > 37$
      $x^2 > 36$ so $x < -6$ *[1 mark]* and $x > 6$ *[1 mark]*
      [2 marks available in total — as above]

4 a) $5 - 3x > 7 - x$, so $-2 > 2x$ *[1 mark]* and $x < -1$ *[1 mark]*
      [2 marks available in total — as above]

   b) 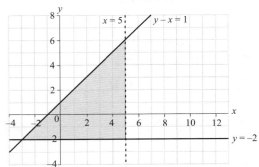 *[1 mark]*

      The circle shouldn't be coloured in — if it was it'd be x ≤ −1.

Page 34: Graphical Inequalities

1 a)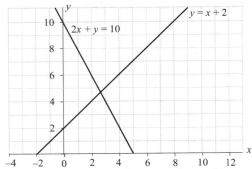
      *[2 marks available — 1 mark for correctly drawing 2x + y = 10,
      1 mark for correctly drawing y = x + 2]*

   b)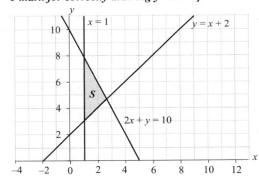
      *[2 marks available — 1 mark for correctly drawing x = 1,
      1 mark for shading the correct area]*

2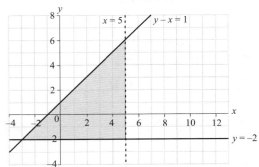
   *[4 marks available — 1 mark for drawing each line correctly,
   1 mark for shading the correct area]*

3 $y \geq 2$ *[1 mark]*, $x + y \leq 8$ *[1 mark]* and $y \leq x$ *[1 mark]*
   [3 marks available in total — as above]

Pages 35: Simultaneous Equations and Graphs

1 $x = 3$ and $y = 4$ *[1 mark]*
   These are the x and y coordinates of the point where the two lines cross.

2 a) $x = 1, y = 2$ *[1 mark]*
   b)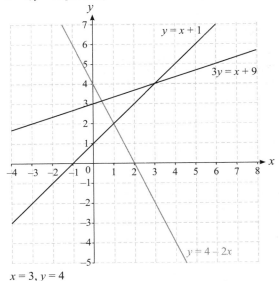

   $x = 3, y = 4$
   *[2 marks available — 1 mark for correctly drawing the
   line 3y = x + 9, 1 mark for the correct answer]*

3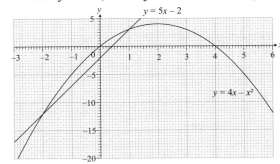

   $x = 1, y = 3$ and $x = -2, y = -12$
   *[3 marks available — 1 mark for correctly drawing
   the line y = 5x − 2, 1 mark for each correct solution]*

Page 36: Simultaneous Equations

1 $x + 3y = 11 \xrightarrow{\times 3} 3x + 9y = 33$ *[1 mark]*

   $3x + 9y = 33$ $x + 3y = 11$
   $\underline{3x + \ y = 9 \ -}$ $x + (3 \times 3) = 11$
    $8y = 24$ $x = 11 - 9$
     $y = 3$ *[1 mark]* $x = 2$ *[1 mark]*
   [3 marks available in total — as above]

2 $2x + 3y = 12 \xrightarrow{\times 5} 10x + 15y = 60$ *[1 mark]*
   $5x + 4y = 9 \xrightarrow{\times 2} 10x + 8y = 18$ *[1 mark]*

   $10x + 15y = 60$ $2x + 3y = 12$
   $\underline{10x + \ 8y = 18 \ -}$ $2x = 12 - (3 \times 6)$
     $7y = 42$ $2x = -6$
      $y = 6$ *[1 mark]* $x = -3$ *[1 mark]*
   [4 marks available in total — as above]

3 $x^2 + y = 4$, so $y = 4 - x^2$
   $4x - 1 = 4 - x^2$ *[1 mark]*
   $x^2 + 4x - 5 = 0$ *[1 mark]*
   $(x + 5)(x - 1) = 0$ *[1 mark]*
   $x = -5$ or $x = 1$ *[1 mark]*

   When $x = 1$, $y = (4 \times 1) - 1 = 3$
   When $x = -5$, $y = (4 \times -5) - 1 = -21$

   So the solutions are $x = 1, y = 3$ and $x = -5, y = -21$ *[1 mark]*
   [5 marks available in total — as above]

Answers

4 $y = x + 6$, so $2x^2 + (x + 6)^2 = 51$ *[1 mark]*
$2x^2 + x^2 + 12x + 36 = 51$
$3x^2 + 12x - 15 = 0$ *[1 mark]*
$(3x - 3)(x + 5) = 0$ *[1 mark]*
$x = 1$ or $x = -5$ *[1 mark]*
When $x = 1$, $y = 1 + 6 = 7$
When $x = -5$, $y = -5 + 6 = 1$
So the solutions are $x = 1$, $y = 7$ *[1 mark]* and $x = -5$, $y = 1$ *[1 mark]*
[6 marks available in total — as above]

Pages 37-38: Direct and Inverse Proportion

1 **a)** $x \propto y^3$, so $x = ky^3$ *[1 mark]*
When $x = 54$ and $y = 3$, $54 = k \times 3^3$,
so $k = 54 \div 3^3 = 54 \div 27 = 2$ *[1 mark]*
So $x = 2y^3$ *[1 mark]*
[3 marks available in total — as above]

    b) $x = 2y^3$ so when $y = 4$, $x = 2 \times 4^3 = 2 \times 64 = 128$ *[1 mark]*

2 **a)** $c \propto \dfrac{1}{d^2}$, so $c = \dfrac{k}{d^2}$ *[1 mark]*
When $c = 2$ and $d = 3$, $2 = \dfrac{k}{3^2}$, so $k = 2 \times 3^2 = 18$ *[1 mark]*
So $c = \dfrac{18}{d^2}$ *[1 mark]*
[3 marks available in total — as above]

    b) $c = \dfrac{18}{d^2}$ so when $c = 0.5$, $0.5 = \dfrac{18}{d^2}$, $d = \pm\sqrt{\dfrac{18}{0.5}}$ *[1 mark]*
$= \pm 6$ *[1 mark]*
[2 marks available in total — as above]

3 **a)** $A \propto \sqrt{T}$, so $A = k\sqrt{T}$ *[1 mark]*
When $T = 36$ and $A = 4$, $4 = k\sqrt{36}$, so $k = 4 \div \sqrt{36} = \dfrac{2}{3}$ *[1 mark]*
So $A = \dfrac{2}{3}\sqrt{T}$ *[1 mark]*
[3 marks available in total — as above]

    b)   If T halves, $\sqrt{T}$ will be divided by $\sqrt{2}$.
A is directly proportional to $\sqrt{T}$, so the value of A must also be
divided by $\sqrt{2}$. *[1 mark]*

4 **a)** $S \propto \dfrac{1}{d}$, so $S = \dfrac{k}{d}$ *[1 mark]*
When $S = 60$ and $d = 15$, $60 = \dfrac{k}{15}$, so $k = 900$ *[1 mark]*
So $S = \dfrac{900}{d}$ *[1 mark]*
[3 marks available in total — as above]

    b)

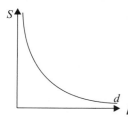

[1 mark]

5 **a)** $x \propto M$, so $x = kM$ *[1 mark]*
When $M = 40$ and $x = 2$, $2 = k \times 40$, so $k = 2 \div 40 = \dfrac{1}{20}$ *[1 mark]*
So $x = \dfrac{1}{20}M$ or $M = 20x$ *[1 mark]*
[3 marks available in total — as above]

    b) $x = \dfrac{1}{20}M$ so when $M = 55$, $x = \dfrac{1}{20} \times 55 = 2.75$ cm *[1 mark]*

6 **a)** $h \propto S^2$, so $h = kS^2$ *[1 mark]*
When $h = 35$ and $S = 50$, $35 = k \times 50^2$,
so $k = 35 \div 50^2 = 0.014$ *[1 mark]*
So $h = 0.014S^2$ *[1 mark]*
[3 marks available in total — as above]

    b) $h = 0.014S^2$ so when $S = 40$, $h = 0.014 \times 40^2 = 22.4$ *[1 mark]*

Section Three — Graphs, Functions and Calculus

Pages 39-40: Straight Line Graphs

1

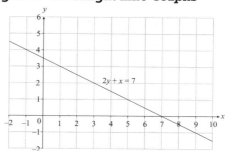

*[3 marks available — 1 mark for plotting any point on the line
(e.g. (0, 3.5)), 1 mark for plotting a second correct point
(e.g. (7, 0)), 1 mark for the correct line extending between
$x = -2$ and $x = 10$]*
*To draw these graphs, you could either create a table of values and
plot the points, or you could set y = 0 and x = 0 and join up the points.*

2 **a)** $\left(\dfrac{(6 + (-4))}{2}, \dfrac{(2 + 1)}{2} \right)$ *[1 mark]*
$= (1, 1.5)$ *[1 mark]*
[2 marks available in total — as above]

    b) $\dfrac{(6 + a)}{2} = 3$
$a = 6 - 6$
$a = 0$
$\dfrac{2 + b}{2} = 5$
$b = 10 - 2$
$b = 8$
*[3 marks available — 1 mark for a correct method and 1 mark
for each correct a and b value]*

3 **a)**   Gradient $= \dfrac{\text{change in } y}{\text{change in } x} = \dfrac{(7 - (-3))}{(5 - 0)}$ *[1 mark]*
$= 2$ *[1 mark]*
[2 marks available in total — as above]

    b)   Using $y = mx + c$ and $m = 2$ gives $y = 2x + c$.
When $x = 0$ and $y = -3$, $-3 = (2 \times 0) + c \Rightarrow c = -3$
So, $y = 2x - 3$ *[1 mark]*

    c)   Using gradient from part a), $m = 2$ *[1 mark]*
When $x = 2$, $y = 10$, so
$10 = (2 \times 2) + c$
i.e. $c = 6$
So, $y = 2x + 6$ *[1 mark]*
[2 marks available in total — as above]

4 **a)** $4y - 5x = 8$
$4y = 5x + 8$ *[1 mark]*
$y = \dfrac{5}{4}x + 2$ *[1 mark]* so the gradient is $\dfrac{5}{4}$ (or 1.25). *[1 mark]*
[3 marks available in total — as above]

    b)   Solve the equations simultaneously:
$4y - 5x = 8 \xrightarrow{\times 3} 12y - 15x = 24$ *[1 mark]*
$3y - 2x = 20 \xrightarrow{\times 4} 12y - 8x = 80$ *[1 mark]*

$\begin{aligned} 12y - 15x &= 24 \\ \underline{12y - 8x} &= \underline{80} \; - \\ -7x &= -56 \\ x &= 8 \end{aligned}$ *[1 mark]* $\begin{aligned} 3y - 2x &= 20 \\ 3y - (2 \times 8) &= 20 \\ 3y &= 36 \\ y &= 12 \end{aligned}$ *[1 mark]*

So the coordinates of point M are (8, 12). *[1 mark]*
[5 marks available in total — as above]
*You could also rearrange the original equations to eliminate x
or substitute one into the other.*

130

Pages 41-42: Harder Graphs

1   a)

x	2.5	3	3.5	4
y	−5.375	−5	−2.125	4

*[2 marks available — 2 marks for all answers correct,
otherwise 1 mark for two correct answers]*

b)

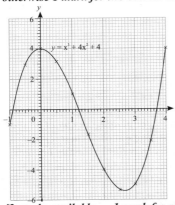

*[2 marks available — 1 mark for plotting correct points,
1 mark for joining them with a smooth curve]*

c)   Reading off the graph, where the line intersects the x-axis,
$x = -0.9$, $x = 1.2$ and $x = 3.7$ *[1 mark]*
You'll still get the mark if your answers are within 0.1 of the answer.

d) $x^3 - 4x^2 + 2 = 0$
$x^3 - 4x^2 + 4 = 2$ so draw the line of $y = 2$ on the graph and
find the solutions where this line intersects the curve:
$x = -0.7$, $x = 0.8$ and $x = 3.9$
*[2 marks available — 1 mark for drawing the line y = 2 on the
graph, 1 mark for the correct solutions]*
You'll still get the mark if your answers are within 0.1 of the answer.

2   a)

x	0.2	5
y	17.2	2.8

[1 mark]

b)

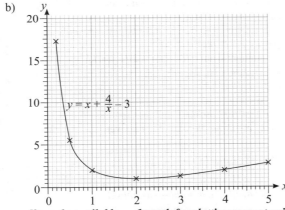

*[2 marks available — 1 mark for plotting correct points,
1 mark for joining them with a smooth curve]*

c) $x + \dfrac{4}{x} - 5.5 = 0$

$x + \dfrac{4}{x} - 3 = 2.5$ so draw the line of $y = 2.5$ on the graph and
find the solutions where this line intersects the curve:
$x = 0.9$ and $x = 4.6$
*[2 marks available — 1 mark for drawing the line y = 2.5
on the graph, 1 mark for the correct solutions]*
You'll still get the mark if your answers are within 0.1 of the answer.

d)   Draw the line of $y = x$ on the graph and find the solution where
this line intersects the curve: $x = 1.3$.
*[2 marks available — 1 mark for drawing the line y = x on the
graph, 1 mark for the correct solution]*
You'll still get the mark if your answers are within 0.1 of the answer.

Pages 43-44: Functions

1   a) $f(7.5) = \dfrac{3}{2(7.5) + 5} = \dfrac{3}{20} = 0.15$ *[1 mark]*

b) $2x + 5 = 0$
$2x = -5$
$x = -2.5$ must be excluded from the domain. *[1 mark]*

c)   Write out $x = f(y)$, $x = \dfrac{3}{2y + 5}$ *[1 mark]*
Rearrange to make y the subject:
$2y + 5 = \dfrac{3}{x}$
$2y = \dfrac{3}{x} - 5$ *[1 mark]*
$y = \dfrac{3}{2x} - \dfrac{5}{2}$ so $f^{-1}(x) = \dfrac{3}{2x} - \dfrac{5}{2}$ *[1 mark]*
[3 marks available in total — as above]

2   a) $g(21) = \sqrt{2 \times 21 - 6} = \sqrt{36} = 6$ *[1 mark]*

b) $gf(x) = g(f(x)) = \sqrt{2(2x^2 + 3) - 6}$ *[1 mark]*
$= \sqrt{4x^2 + 6 - 6}$
$= \sqrt{4x^2}$
$= 2x$ *[1 mark]*
[2 marks available in total — as above]

c) $fg(a) = f(g(a)) = 2(\sqrt{2a - 6})^2 + 3$ *[1 mark]*
$= 2(2a - 6) + 3$
$= 4a - 9$ *[1 mark]*
So when $fg(a) = 7$, $4a - 9 = 7$
$a = 4$ *[1 mark]*
[3 marks available in total — as above]

3   a) $f(13) = \sqrt{13^2 - 25} = \sqrt{169 - 25} = \sqrt{144} = 12$ *[1 mark]*

b) $x^2 - 25 < 0$ *[1 mark]*
$x^2 < 25$
$-5 < x < 5$ *[1 mark]*
[2 marks available in total — as above]

c)   If $f(x) = 1$, $\sqrt{x^2 - 25} = 1$ *[1 mark]*
$x^2 - 25 = 1^2$ *[1 mark]*
$x^2 = 1 + 25$
$x = \pm\sqrt{26}$ *[1 mark]*
[3 marks available in total — as above]

d)   Reading from the graph $g(1) = -10$ *[1 mark]*
$fg(1) = f(g(1)) = f(-10) = \sqrt{(-10)^2 - 25} = \sqrt{75}$ *[1 mark]*
[2 marks available in total — as above]

Pages 45-46: Differentiation

1   $\dfrac{dy}{dx} = 6x^2 + 2x - 8$
*[2 marks available — 2 marks for the correct answer,
otherwise 1 mark for differentiating 1 term correctly]*

2   a) $\dfrac{dy}{dx} = -2x$ *[1 mark]*

b)   At $x = -1$: $\dfrac{dy}{dx} = -2(-1) = 2$ *[1 mark]*
At $x = 2$: $\dfrac{dy}{dx} = -2(2) = -4$ *[1 mark]*
[2 marks available in total — as above]

3   a) $y = 3x^2 + \dfrac{7}{2}x^{-1}$
$\dfrac{dy}{dx} = 6x - \dfrac{7}{2}x^{-2}$
$= 6x - \dfrac{7}{2x^2}$
*[3 marks available — 1 mark for the '6x' term,
2 marks for the '$\dfrac{7}{2x^2}$' term]*

Answers

b) At a turning point $\frac{dy}{dx} = 0$, so

$6x - \frac{7}{2x^2} = 0$ *[1 mark]*

$6x = \frac{7}{2x^2}$

$12x^3 = 7$

$x^3 = \frac{7}{12}$ *[1 mark]*

$x = 0.8355... = 0.84$ (2 d.p.) *[1 mark]*

$y = 3(0.8355...)^2 + \frac{7}{2 \times 0.8355...} = 6.2832...$

$\qquad\qquad\qquad\qquad\qquad = 6.28$ (2 d.p.) *[1 mark]*

So the coordinates of the turning point are (0.84, 6.28).
[4 marks available in total — as above]

4 $h = -2x^2 + 15x + 12$

$\frac{dh}{dx} = -4x + 15$ *[2 marks — 1 mark for each correct term]*

Maximum is at $\frac{dh}{dx} = 0$, so

$-4x + 15 = 0$ *[1 mark]*

$-4x = -15$

$x = 3.75$ *[1 mark]*

$h = -2 \times 3.75^2 + (15 \times 3.75) + 12 = 40.125$ m *[1 mark]*
[5 marks available in total — as above]

5 a) $A = (5x + 1)(5 - 2x)$ *[1 mark]*

$= -10x^2 + 25x - 2x + 5$

$= -10x^2 + 23x + 5$ *[1 mark]*
[2 marks available in total — as above]

b) $\frac{dA}{dx} = -20x + 23$

[2 marks available — 1 mark for each correct term]

c) Maximum is at $\frac{dA}{dx} = 0$, so

$-20x + 23 = 0$ *[1 mark]*

$-20x = -23$

$x = 1.15$ *[1 mark]*

$A = -10 \times 1.15^2 + (23 \times 1.15) + 5 = 18.225$ km^2 *[1 mark]*
[3 marks available in total — as above]

6 a) $s = 2t^3 - 3t^2 + 8$

$v = \frac{ds}{dt} = 6t^2 - 6t$ *[2 marks — 1 mark for each correct term]*

When $t = 4$, $v = (6 \times 4^2) - (6 \times 4) = 72$ m/s *[1 mark]*
[3 marks available in total — as above]

b) $a = \frac{dv}{dt} = 12t - 6$ *[1 mark]*

When $a = 0$,

$0 = 12t - 6$ *[1 mark]*

$6 = 12t$

$t = 0.5$ seconds *[1 mark]*
[3 marks available in total — as above]

Section Four — Geometry and Measures

Pages 47-48: Geometry

1 Angle BCA = angle BAC *[1 mark]*
Angle BCA = $(180° - 48°) \div 2 = 66°$ *[1 mark]*
Angle BCD = $180° - 66° = 114°$ *[1 mark]*
[3 marks available in total — as above]

2 Angle CBE = $180° - 115° = 65°$ *[1 mark]*
Angle DEB = $180° - 103° = 77°$ *[1 mark]*
Angle x = $360° - 65° - 77° - 90° = 128°$ *[1 mark]*
[3 marks available in total — as above]

3 a) Angles on a straight line add up to 180°,
so angle FEC = $180° - 14° = 166°$ *[1 mark]*
Angles in a quadrilateral add up to 360°,
so x = $360° - 90° - 62° - 166° = 42°$ *[1 mark]*
[2 marks available in total — as above]

b) Angles in a triangle add up to 180° *[1 mark]*
so y = $180° - 90° - 42° = 48°$ *[1 mark]*
[2 marks available in total — as above]

4 Angle ABJ = $180° - 140° = 40°$ *[1 mark]*
Angle JAB = $180° - 150° = 30°$ *[1 mark]*
Angle AJB = $180° - 40° - 30° = 110°$ *[1 mark]*
Angle x = $180° - 110° = 70°$ *[1 mark]*
[4 marks available in total — as above]

5 $5x + (4x - 9°) = 180°$ *[1 mark]*
Rearranging this: $9x = 189°$
Therefore $x = 21°$ *[1 mark]*
$(4y - 12°) + 2y = 180°$ *[1 mark]*
Rearranging this: $6y = 192°$
Therefore $y = 32°$ *[1 mark]*
[4 marks available in total — as above]

6 Angles on a straight line add up to 180°,
so angle ADO = $180° - 142° = 38°$ *[1 mark]*
Angles in a triangle add up to 180°,
so angle AOD = $180° - 38° - 90° = 52°$ *[1 mark]*
OCB is an isosceles triangle so angle OBC = angle OCB = 27°,
so angle COB = $180° - 27° - 27° = 126°$ *[1 mark]*
angle AOC = angle AOD + angle COB = $52° + 126° = 178°$ *[1 mark]*
[4 marks available in total — as above]

Pages 49-50: Polygons

1 Exterior angle = $180° - 150° = 30°$ *[1 mark]*
Number of sides = $360° \div 30°$ *[1 mark]*
= 12 *[1 mark]*
[3 marks available in total — as above]

2 Exterior angle of a pentagon = $360° \div 5 = 72°$
Interior angle of a pentagon = $180° - 72° = 108°$
Angle in an equilateral triangle = $180° \div 3 = 60°$
p = $360° - (108° + 60°)$ *(angles round a point add up to 360°)*
$= 360° - 168° = 192°$
[3 marks available — 1 mark for calculating the interior angle of the pentagon, 1 mark for calculating the angle of the triangle, 1 mark for the correct final answer]

3 a) x is the same as an exterior angle, so $x = 360° \div 8$ *[1 mark]*
$x = 45°$ *[1 mark]*
[2 marks available in total — as above]

b) $y = (180° - 45°) \div 2$ *[1 mark]*
$y = 67.5°$ *[1 mark]*
[2 marks available in total — as above]

4 Sum of interior angles in a heptagon = $(7 - 2) \times 180°$ *[1 mark]*
$= 900°$ *[1 mark]*
Sum of the known angles
$= 137° + 128° + 109° + 152° + 134° + 140° = 800°$ *[1 mark]*
$x = 900° - 800° = 100°$ *[1 mark]*
[4 marks available in total — as above]
You can also find the sum of the interior angles using the formula $(2n - 4) \times 90°$.

5 Angles DEF and EFG add up to 180° as they are allied angles,
so angle EFG = $180° - 151° = 29°$ *[1 mark]*
Angles around a point add up to 360°,
so angle AFE = $360° - 224° = 136°$
Angle AFG = angle AFE − angle EFG = $136° - 29° = 107°$ *[1 mark]*
Angles x and AFG add up to 180° as they are allied angles,
so x = $180° - 107° = 73°$ *[1 mark]*
Sum of interior angles in a hexagon = $(6 - 2) \times 180° = 720°$ *[1 mark]*
Sum of the known angles = $117° + 151° + 136° + 73° + 137°$
$= 614°$ *[1 mark]*
$y = 720° - 614° = 106°$ *[1 mark]*
[6 marks available in total — as above]

6 Exterior angle = $360° \div 18 = 20°$ *[1 mark]*
Interior angle = $180° - 20° = 160°$ *[1 mark]*
The interior angles cannot be made to add up to 360°, so 18-sided regular polygons do not tessellate. *[1 mark]*
[3 marks available in total — as above]

Pages 51-53: Circle Geometry

1 a) Angle $BCD = 150° \div 2 = 75°$ *[1 mark]*
    (Angle at the centre is 2 × angle at circumference.) *[1 mark]*
    [2 marks available in total — as above]

  b) Opposite angles in a cyclic quadrilateral sum to 180°. *[1 mark]*

2 Angle $DBC = 62°$ *[1 mark]*
  Angle $ABC = 90°$ *[1 mark]*
  Angle $x = 90° - 62° = 28°$ *[1 mark]*
  [3 marks available in total — as above]

3 x = angle $EAC = 37°$ *[1 mark]* and y = angle $DAB = 79°$ *[1 mark]*
  because of the alternate segment theorem. *[1 mark]*
  [3 marks available in total — as above]
  Once you've found one angle you can also use angles on a straight line
  and angles in a triangle to find the other one.

4 a) $x = 28°$ *[1 mark]* $y = 24°$ *[1 mark]*
    [2 marks available in total — as above]

  b) Angles in the same segment are equal. *[1 mark]*

5 Angles ODE and OBE are both 90°. *[1 mark]*
  Angle $DOB = 360° - 90° - 90° - 80° = 100°$. *[1 mark]*
  Angle $DCB = 100° \div 2 = 50°$. *[1 mark]*
  Angle $DAB = 180° - 50° = 130°$. *[1 mark]*
  [4 marks available in total — as above]

6 Using the external intersection of two chords property:
  $AC \times AB = AD \times AE$
  $(10 + 6) \times 6 = (8 + x) \times 8$ *[1 mark]*
  $96 = 64 + 8x$
  So $x = 4$ cm *[1 mark]*
  [2 marks available in total — as above]

7 BO is the perpendicular bisector of the chord AD,
  so $FD = AF = 6$ cm *[1 mark]*
  Using the internal intersection of two chords property:
  $AF \times FD = CF \times FE$ *[1 mark]*
  $6 \times 6 = CF \times 9$
  $CF = 4$ cm *[1 mark]*
  [3 marks available in total — as above]

8 Angle $DCO = 90°$ *[1 mark]*
  Angle $DOC = 180° - 90° - 24° = 66°$ *[1 mark]*
  Angle $AOC = 66° \times 2 = 132°$ *[1 mark]*
  Angle $ABC = 66°$ *[1 mark]*
  Angle $CBE = 180° - 66° = 114°$ *[1 mark]*
  [5 marks available in total — as above]

Pages 54-55: The Four Transformations

1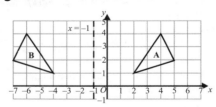

[2 marks available — 2 marks for shape correctly reflected and in the right place on the grid, otherwise 1 mark for shape correctly reflected but in wrong location]

2 a) and b)

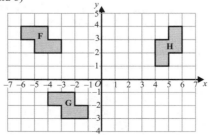

[1 mark available for part a) for correct translation]
[2 marks available for part b) — 1 mark for a rotation of 90° clockwise around any point, 1 mark for correct centre of rotation]

3 a) Rotation 90° anti-clockwise around the point (0, 0)
    [3 marks available — 1 mark for rotation, 1 mark for correct angle and direction of rotation, 1 mark for correct centre of rotation]

  b)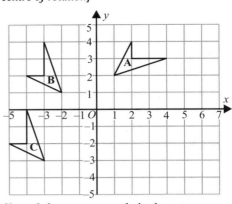

[1 mark for correct translation]

4 a) and b)

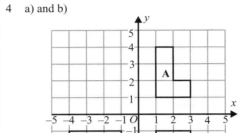

[2 marks available for part a) — 2 marks if shape correctly reflected and in the right place on the grid, otherwise 1 mark if shape correctly reflected but in wrong location]
[2 marks available for part b) — 1 mark for a rotation of 90° clockwise around any point, 1 mark for the correct centre of rotation]

  c) Reflection in the line $y = -x$ *[2 marks available — 1 mark for reflection, 1 mark for correct line of reflection]*

5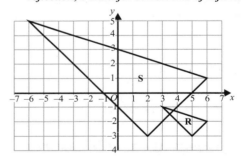

[3 marks available — 1 mark for any enlargement, 1 mark for enlarging by scale factor 4, 1 mark for correct position]

6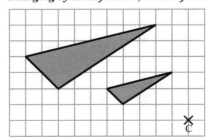

[3 marks available — 1 mark for any enlargement, 1 mark for enlarging by scale factor $\frac{1}{2}$, 1 mark for correct position]

Answers

Page 56: More Transformation Stuff

1 Area of enlarged shape = 7×3^2 *[1 mark]*
   = 63 cm² *[1 mark]*
   [2 marks available in total — as above]

2 Scale factor = $5 \div 2 = 2.5$ *[1 mark]*
   Enlarged area = $6 \times 2.5^2 = 37.5$ cm² *[1 mark]*
   [2 marks available in total — as above]
   Remember that you have to square the scale factor when you're scaling up areas.

3 $1^3 : 7^3 = 1 : 343$ *[1 mark]*

4 a) Scale factor from **A** to **C**:
     $n^2 = 108\pi \div 12\pi = 9$ *[1 mark]*
     $n = 3$ *[1 mark]*
     Volume of **A** = 135π cm³ $\div 3^3$ *[1 mark]*
     = 5π cm³ *[1 mark]*
     [4 marks available in total — as above]

   b) Scale factor from **A** to **B**:
     $m^2 = 48\pi \div 12\pi = 4$ *[1 mark]*
     $m = 2$ *[1 mark]*
     Perpendicular height of **B** = 4 cm × 2 *[1 mark]*
     = 8 cm *[1 mark]*
     [4 marks available in total — as above]

Page 57-58: Similarity

1 a) Scale factor from *DEF* to *ABC* = $30 \div 12 = 2.5$ *[1 mark]*
     AB = $7 \times 2.5 = 17.5$ cm *[1 mark]*
     [2 marks available in total — as above]

   b) *DF* = $35 \div 2.5 = 14$ cm *[1 mark]*

2 a) Scale factor from *EFGH* to *ABCD* = $9 \div 6 = 1.5$ *[1 mark]*
     BC = $4 \times 1.5 = 6$ cm *[1 mark]*
     [2 marks available in total — as above]

   b) *EF* = $6 \div 1.5 = 4$ cm *[1 mark]*

   c) Corresponding angles are equal in similar shapes so:
     x = angle *ADC* = $360° - 42° - 112° - 79° = 127°$ *[1 mark]*

   d) $36 \div (1.5)^2 = 16$ cm²
     [2 marks available — 1 mark for using the correct scale factor (1.5²), 1 mark for the correct answer]

3 a) 1.5 m = 150 cm, so the scale factor from the small banner to the large banner = $150 \div 30 = 5$ *[1 mark]*
     $x = 40 \div 5 = 8$ cm *[1 mark]*
     [2 marks available in total — as above]

   b) $0.6 \div (5)^2 = 0.024$ m²
     [2 marks available — 1 mark for using the correct scale factor (5²), 1 mark for the correct answer]

4 a) The scale factor from *ABC* to *CDE* = $18 \div 4.5 = 4$ *[1 mark]*
     BC = $12 \div 4 = 3$ cm *[1 mark]*
     [2 marks available in total — as above]

   b) *CD* = $4 \times 4 = 16$ cm *[1 mark]*
     AD = *AC* + *CD* = $4 + 16 = 20$ cm *[1 mark]*
     [2 marks available in total — as above]

5 a) The scale factor from *ABC* to *ACD* = $8 \div 6 = \frac{4}{3}$ *[1 mark]*
     $x = 6 \div \frac{4}{3} = 4.5$ cm *[1 mark]*
     $y = 3 \times \frac{4}{3} = 4$ cm *[1 mark]*
     [3 marks available in total — as above]

   b) $9 \times \left(\frac{4}{3}\right)^2 = 16$ cm²
     [2 marks available — 1 mark for using the correct scale factor $\left(\frac{4}{3}\right)^2$, 1 mark for the correct answer]

Pages 59-60: Areas and Perimeters

1 Area of field = $\frac{1}{2} \times (105 + 80) \times 60 = 5550$ m²
   [2 marks available — 1 mark for putting the numbers into the formula correctly, 1 mark for the correct answer]

2 a) Flowerbed area = $\frac{\pi \times 5^2}{2}$ m² and patio area = $\frac{\pi \times 5^2}{2}$ m²
     Lawn area = $(30 \times 10) - \frac{\pi \times 5^2}{2} - \frac{\pi \times 5^2}{2}$
     = 221.4601... m² = 221.46 m² (to 2 d.p.)
     [3 marks available — 1 mark for working out the areas of the flowerbed and patio, 1 mark for a correct method for finding the lawn area, 1 mark for the correct answer]

   b) Lawn perimeter = 30 m + $\frac{\pi \times 10}{2}$ m + 30 m + $\frac{\pi \times 10}{2}$ m
     = 91.4159... m = 91.42 m (to 2 d.p.)
     [3 marks available — 1 mark for working out the lengths of the curved parts of the lawn, 1 mark for a correct method for finding the perimeter, 1 mark for correct final answer]

3 Area of a parallelogram = base × vertical height
   So, vertical height = area ÷ base = $105 \div 15 = 7$ cm
   [2 marks available — 1 mark for dividing the area by the base, 1 mark for the correct answer]

4 Area of full circle = $\pi \times 12^2 = 144\pi$ cm²
   Area of sector = $(50 \div 360) \times$ area of circle
   = $(50 \div 360) \times 144\pi$ cm²
   = 62.831... cm² = 62.8 cm² (3 s.f.)
   [4 marks available — 1 mark for a correct method for finding the area of the full circle, 1 mark for correct area of the full circle, 1 mark for a correct method for calculating the area of the sector, and 1 mark for the correct answer]

5 Circumference of full circle = $2 \times \pi \times 6 = 12\pi$ cm
   Length of arc = $(30 \div 360) \times$ circumference of circle
   = $(30 \div 360) \times 12\pi = \pi$ cm
   Perimeter of sector = $\pi + 6 + 6 = 15.1$ cm (3 s.f.)
   [4 marks available — 1 mark for a correct method for finding the circumference of the full circle, 1 mark for a correct method for calculating the length of the arc, 1 mark for correct arc length, and 1 mark for the correct answer]

Pages 61-63: Surface Area and Volume

1 Side length of the cube = $\sqrt[3]{729}$ = 9 cm *[1 mark]*
   One face of the cube = $9 \times 9 = 81$ cm² *[1 mark]*
   Total surface area of the cube = $81 \times 6 = 486$ *[1 mark]*
   [3 marks available in total — as above]

2 a) Area of one circular face = $\pi \times 5^2$ *[1 mark]*
     Area of the curved face = $15 \times 10\pi$ *[1 mark]*
     Total surface area = $(15 \times 10\pi) + 2(\pi \times 5^2)$
     = 628.3185... cm²
     = 628 cm² (3 s.f.) *[1 mark]*
     [3 marks available in total — as above]

   b) Volume = $15 \times (5^2 \times \pi)$ *[1 mark]*
     = 1178.097... cm³
     = 1180 cm³ (3 s.f.) *[1 mark]*
     [2 marks available in total — as above]

3 Volume of pool = $\pi \times (2 \div 2)^2 \times 0.4 = 0.4\pi$ m³ *[1 mark]*
   Volume of water Amy should use = $0.4\pi \times \frac{3}{4}$ *[1 mark]*
   = 0.94 m³ (to 2 d.p.) *[1 mark]*
   [3 marks available in total — as above]

4 A regular hexagon is made up of 6 identical triangles.
   Area of triangle = $\frac{1}{2} \times 8 \times 7 = 28$ cm² *[1 mark]*
   Area of whole hexagon cross-section = $28 \times 6 = 168$ cm² *[1 mark]*
   Volume of prism = cross-sectional area × length =
   $168 \times 6 = 1008$ cm³ *[1 mark]*
   [3 marks available in total — as above]

5 Surface area of curved part of hemisphere =
$\frac{1}{2}$ × surface area of a sphere = $\frac{1}{2} \times 4 \times \pi \times 7^2$ *[1 mark]*
= 307.876... cm²
Surface area of curved part of cone = $\pi \times 2 \times 12$ *[1 mark]*
= 75.398... cm²
Surface area of flat top of hemisphere = $(\pi \times 7^2) - (\pi \times 2^2)$ *[1 mark]*
= 141.371... cm²
Total surface area = 307.876... + 75.398... + 141.371...
= 525 cm² (to 3 s.f.) *[1 mark]*
[4 marks available in total — as above]

6 Volume = $\frac{1}{2} \times (\frac{4}{3} \times \pi \times 9^3) - \frac{1}{2} \times (\frac{4}{3} \times \pi \times 8^3)$ *[1 mark]*
= 1526.814... − 1072.330... *[1 mark]*
= 454 cm³ (3 s.f.) *[1 mark]*
[3 marks available in total — as above]
You still get full marks if you simplified the volume before multiplying everything through — e.g. you got $\frac{2}{3}\pi(729 - 512)$.

7 Length of arc = $(90 \div 360) \times (2 \times \pi \times 16) = 8\pi$ *[1 mark]*
The circumference of the base = 8π, so the diameter of the base is $8\pi \div \pi = 8$. The radius is therefore $8 \div 2 = 4$ cm *[1 mark]*
Volume of cone = $\frac{1}{3}(\pi \times 4^2 \times 15.5)$ *[1 mark]*
= 259.704... cm³ = 260 cm³ (3 s.f.) *[1 mark]*
[4 marks available in total — as above]

8 Volume of cone = $\frac{1}{3}(\pi \times 6^2 \times 18) = 216\pi$ cm³ *[1 mark]*
So $\frac{4}{3}\pi r^3 = 216\pi$ cm³ *[1 mark]*
$r^3 = 162$ *[1 mark]*
$r = 5.4513...$ cm = 5.45 cm (3 s.f.) *[1 mark]*
[4 marks available in total — as above]

9 Volume of cuboid = $2r \times 2r \times 4r = 16r^3$ *[1 mark]*
Volume of both spheres = $2 \times \frac{4}{3}\pi r^3 = \frac{8}{3}\pi r^3$ *[1 mark]*
Volume of unoccupied space = $16r^3 - \frac{8}{3}\pi r^3$ *[1 mark]*
[3 marks available in total — as above]

Page 64: Speed

1 a) 1 hour 4 minutes = $1\frac{1}{15}$ hours or 1.0666... hours *[1 mark]*
Speed = $\frac{\text{distance}}{\text{time}}$, so speed = $\frac{6 \text{ km}}{1.0666... \text{ hours}}$ *[1 mark]*
= 5.625 km/h *[1 mark]*
[3 marks available in total — as above]

   b) Time = $\frac{\text{distance}}{\text{speed}}$, so time = $\frac{6 \text{ km}}{25 \text{ km/h}}$ = 0.24 hours
= 14.4 minutes
[3 marks available — 1 mark for using the correct formula, 1 mark for the correct calculation, 1 mark for the correct answer]

2 Distance = speed × time, so distance = 56 × 1.25
= 70 km
[3 marks available — 1 mark for using the correct formula, 1 mark for the correct calculation, 1 mark for the correct answer]

3 In 2014 he finished with a time of $t - 0.1t = 0.9t$ *[1 mark]*
$s_1 = \frac{d}{t}$ and $s_2 = \frac{d}{0.9t}$ *[1 mark]*
So, $s_1 t = 0.9 s_2 t$
$s_2 = \frac{s_1}{0.9} = 1.111... \times s_1$ *[1 mark]*
So his percentage increase was 11.11% (2 d.p.) *[1 mark]*
[4 marks available in total — as above]
There are other methods to get to the correct answer, as long as you show full working and get the answer right then you will get full marks.

Page 65: Distance-Time Graphs

1 a) 15 ÷ 1 *[1 mark]*
= 15 *[1 mark]*
[2 marks available in total — as above]

   b) The speed at which Selby is travelling. *[1 mark]*

   c) 3 hours *[1 mark]*
As he was at point A at O hours, all you have to do is read off the x-value at point C to see how long Selby's journey was.

   d) 2.5 hours *[1 mark]*

   e)

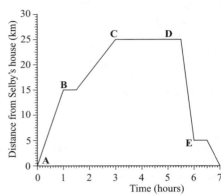

[2 marks available — 1 mark for a flat line from point E for 30 minutes, and 1 mark for a straight line from this point to (7,0)]

   f) 7 − 0.5 − 2.5 − 0.5 = 3.5 hours *[1 mark]*
Selby isn't cycling whenever the graph shows a horizontal line. So, subtract these times from the total amount of time he is out.

Pages 66-67: Constructions

1 a)

[2 marks available — 1 mark for arcs drawn with a radius of 4.5 cm, 1 mark for completed triangle]

   b)

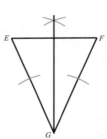

[2 marks available — 1 mark for correct construction arcs, 1 mark for correct bisector]

2

[2 marks available — 1 mark for correct construction arcs, 1 mark for the correct perpendicular bisector of AB]

Answers

3

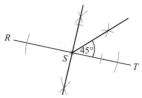

[4 marks available — 1 mark for correct construction arcs for a perpendicular bisector, 1 mark for the correct perpendicular bisector of RT through S, 1 mark for correct construction lines for angle bisector, 1 mark for correct 45° angle]

Here you have to first construct a 90° angle by drawing a perpendicular bisector which passes through midpoint S, then bisect this 90° angle to give the 45° angle. You could bisect any of the four 90° angles formed by the perpendicular bisector.

4

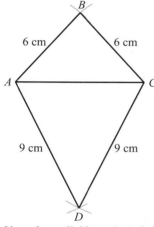

[4 marks available — 1 mark for correct 6 cm construction arcs, 1 mark for correct 9 cm construction arcs, 1 mark for a correctly drawn kite, 1 mark for labelling B and D correctly]

Section Five — Pythagoras and Trigonometry

Page 68: Pythagoras' Theorem

1   $AB^2 = 4^2 + 8^2$ *[1 mark]*
$AB = \sqrt{16 + 64} = \sqrt{80}$ *[1 mark]*
$AB = 8.94$ cm (2 d.p) *[1 mark]*
[3 marks available in total — as above]

2   $3.5^2 = x^2 + 2.1^2$ *[1 mark]*
$x = \sqrt{12.25 - 4.41} = \sqrt{7.84}$ *[1 mark]*
$x = 2.8$ m *[1 mark]*
[3 marks available in total — as above]

3   Let h be the height of the triangle:
$13^2 = 5^2 + h^2$ *[1 mark]*
$h = \sqrt{169 - 25} = \sqrt{144}$ *[1 mark]*
$h = 12$ cm *[1 mark]*
Area, $A = \frac{1}{2} \times 10 \times 12$
$A = 60$ cm^2 *[1 mark]*
[4 marks available in total — as above]

4   Length of EA:
$28.3^2 = 20^2 + EA^2$ *[1 mark]*
$EA = \sqrt{800.89 - 400}$
$EA = 20.02...$ *[1 mark]*
Length of CE:
$54.3^2 = 20^2 + CE^2$ *[1 mark]*
$CE = \sqrt{2948.49 - 400}$
$CE = 50.48...$ *[1 mark]*
Perimeter $= 28.3 + 54.3 + EA + CE = 153.1$ cm (1 d.p) *[1 mark]*
[5 marks available in total — as above]

Pages 69-70: Trigonometry — Sin, Cos, Tan

1   $\sin x = \frac{14}{18}$ *[1 mark]*
$x = \sin^{-1}\left(\frac{14}{18}\right)$ *[1 mark]*
$x = 51.1°$ (1 d.p) *[1 mark]*
[3 marks available in total — as above]

2   $\tan 52° = \frac{4}{y}$ *[1 mark]*
$y = \frac{4}{\tan 52°}$ *[1 mark]*
$y = 3.13$ m (3 s.f) *[1 mark]*
[3 marks available in total — as above]

3   a)   Split ABC into two right-angled triangles, and find half of AC (call it x).
$\cos 34° = \frac{x}{10}$ *[1 mark]*
$x = 10 \times \cos 34°$ *[1 mark]*
$x = 8.29...$
$AC = 8.29... \times 2 = 16.58$ m (2 d.p) *[1 mark]*
[3 marks available in total — as above]

b) $\sin 34° = \frac{h}{10}$ *[1 mark]*
$h = 10 \times \sin 34°$ *[1 mark]*
$h = 5.59$ m (2 d.p) *[1 mark]*
[3 marks available in total — as above]
You could also use $\tan 34° = \frac{h}{8.29}$ to work out the answer.

4   Find diameter of the circle: $\tan 58° = \frac{XY}{4}$ *[1 mark]*
$XY = 4\tan 58°$
$XY = 6.4013...$ cm *[1 mark]*

Find length YZ: $\sin 35° = \frac{YZ}{6.4013...}$ *[1 mark]*
$YZ = \sin 35° \times 6.4013...$
$YZ = 3.67$ cm (2 d.p.) *[1 mark]*
[4 marks available in total — as above]

5   a) $\tan x = \frac{6}{9}$ *[1 mark]*
$x = \tan^{-1}\left(\frac{6}{9}\right)$ *[1 mark]*
$x = 33.7°$ (1 d.p) *[1 mark]*
[3 marks available in total — as above]

b)   EG bisects the angle FEH, so find angle FEM:
$\tan x = \frac{6}{5}$ *[1 mark]*
$x = \tan^{-1}\left(\frac{6}{5}\right)$ *[1 mark]*
$x = 50.19...°$
$FEH = 50.19... \times 2 = 100.4°$ (1 d.p) *[1 mark]*
[3 marks available in total — as above]

6   Call the distance from the centre of the circle to the centre of an edge, x. The radius bisects the internal angle forming angle a.

Sum of the internal angles of a hexagon $= 4 \times 180° = 720°$
Each internal angle of a hexagon $= 720° \div 6 = 120°$ *[1 mark]*
$a = 120 \div 2 = 60°$ *[1 mark]*
$\sin 60° = \frac{x}{8.5}$ *[1 mark]*
$x = 8.5 \times \sin 60°$ *[1 mark]*
$x = 7.36$ cm (2 d.p) *[1 mark]*
[5 marks available in total — as above]
You could also use the calculation $\cos 30° \times 8.5$ to find the value of x. As long as you make sure you show your working, you'll get full marks if your answer is correct.

Answers

Pages 71-73: The Sine and Cosine Rules

1 a) $AC^2 = 10^2 + 7^2 - (2 \times 10 \times 7 \times \cos 85°)$ *[1 mark]*
   $AC = \sqrt{149 - 140 \times \cos 85°}$ *[1 mark]*
   $AC = 11.7$ cm (3 s.f) *[1 mark]*
   [3 marks available in total — as above]

   b) Area $= \frac{1}{2} \times 10 \times 7 \times \sin 85°$ *[1 mark]*
   Area $= 34.9$ cm² (3 s.f) *[1 mark]*
   [2 marks available in total — as above]

2 a) $\frac{BD}{\sin 30°} = \frac{8}{\sin 70°}$ *[1 mark]*
   $BD = \frac{8}{\sin 70°} \times \sin 30°$ *[1 mark]*
   $BD = 4.2567...$ m $= 4.26$ m (3 s.f) *[1 mark]*
   [3 marks available in total — as above]

   b) $\frac{4}{\sin BDC} = \frac{4.2567...}{\sin 60°}$ *[1 mark]*
   $\sin BDC = \frac{\sin 60°}{4.2567...} \times 4$

   Angle $BDC = \sin^{-1}(0.813...)$ *[1 mark]*
   Angle $BDC = 54.4°$ (3 s.f) *[1 mark]*
   [3 marks available in total — as above]

3 Angle $ABD = 180° - 90° - 31° - 12° = 47°$

   Angle $ACB = 180° - 12° - 47° = 121°$ *[1 mark]*
   Use the sine rule: $\frac{3.3}{\sin 12°} = \frac{AB}{\sin 121°}$ *[1 mark]*
   $AB = \frac{3.3}{\sin 12°} \times \sin 121°$ *[1 mark]*
   $AB = 13.6050...$ m *[1 mark]*
   Find length BD: $\cos 47° = \frac{BD}{13.6050...}$ *[1 mark]*
   $BD = \cos 47° \times 13.6050...$
   $BD = 9.2786... = 9.28$ m (3 s.f) *[1 mark]*
   [6 marks available in total — as above]

   There's more than one way of doing this question. As long as you've used a correct method to get the right answer you'll still get the marks.

4 *First you need to find one angle using the cosine rule.*
   E.g. use angle CAB.
   $\cos A = \frac{14^2 + 12^2 - 19^2}{2 \times 14 \times 12}$ *[1 mark]*
   $A = \cos^{-1}\left(\frac{-21}{336}\right)$ *[1 mark]*
   $A = 93.58...°$ *[1 mark]*
   Area $= \frac{1}{2} \times 14 \times 12 \times \sin 93.58...°$ *[1 mark]*
   Area $= 83.84$ cm² (2 d.p) *[1 mark]*
   [5 marks available in total — as above]

5 First, split $ABCD$ into two triangles, ABC and ACD.
   $\frac{55}{\sin ACB} = \frac{93}{\sin 116°}$ *[1 mark]*
   $\sin ACB = \frac{\sin 116°}{93} \times 55$ *[1 mark]*
   Angle $ACB = \sin^{-1}(0.531...)$
   $ACB = 32.109...°$ *[1 mark]*
   Angle $BAC = 180° - 116° - 32.109...°$ so,
   Area of $ABC = \frac{1}{2} \times 93 \times 55 \times \sin(180 - 116 - 32.10...)°$ *[1 mark]*
   Area of $ABC = 1351.106...$cm² *[1 mark]*
   Angle $ACD = 78° - 32.109...°$ so
   Area of $ACD = \frac{1}{2} \times 93 \times 84 \times \sin(78 - 32.10...)°$ *[1 mark]*
   Area of $ACD = 2804.531...$cm² *[1 mark]*
   Area of $ABCD = 1351.106... + 2804.531... = 4160$ cm² *[1 mark]*
   [8 marks available in total — as above]

Page 74: 3D Pythagoras and Trigonometry

1 a) $FD^2 = 8^2 + 2^2 + 5^2$ *[1 mark]*
   $FD = \sqrt{93}$ *[1 mark]*
   So maximum length of stick $= 9.6$ cm (2 s.f) *[1 mark]*
   [3 marks available in total — as above]

   b) $\sin FDG = \frac{5}{\sqrt{93}}$ *[1 mark]*
   $FDG = \sin^{-1}\left(\frac{5}{\sqrt{93}}\right)$
   $FDG = 31°$ (2 s.f.) *[1 mark]*
   [2 marks available in total — as above]

2 Find length DC: $5^2 - (7 - 4)^2 = DC^2$ *[1 mark]*
   $DC^2 = 16$
   $DC = 4$ cm
   Find length DG: $4^2 + 11^2 = DG^2$ *[1 mark]*
   $DG^2 = 137$
   $DG = 11.704...$ cm *[1 mark]*
   Find angle AGD: $\tan AGD = \frac{7}{11.704...}$ *[1 mark]*
   $AGD = \tan^{-1}\left(\frac{7}{11.704...}\right)$
   $AGD = 30.9°$ (3 s.f.) *[1 mark]*
   [5 marks available in total — as above]

Page 75: Vectors

1 a) $\overrightarrow{CD} = -2\mathbf{a}$ *[1 mark]*
   b) $\overrightarrow{AC} = 2\mathbf{d} + 2\mathbf{a}$ *[1 mark]*
   c) $\overrightarrow{BL} = \mathbf{d} - \mathbf{a}$ *[1 mark]*

2 a) $\overrightarrow{OM} = \overrightarrow{OA} + \overrightarrow{AM} = \overrightarrow{OA} + \frac{1}{2}\overrightarrow{AB}$ *[1 mark]*
   $\overrightarrow{AB} = \mathbf{b} - 2\mathbf{a}$ or $-2\mathbf{a} + \mathbf{b}$
   $\overrightarrow{OM} = 2\mathbf{a} + \frac{1}{2}(-2\mathbf{a} + \mathbf{b})$ or $\overrightarrow{OM} = 2\mathbf{a} + \frac{1}{2}(\mathbf{b} - 2\mathbf{a})$
   $= \mathbf{a} + \frac{1}{2}\mathbf{b}$ *[1 mark]*
   [2 marks available in total — as above]

   b) $\overrightarrow{OX} = \overrightarrow{OA} + \overrightarrow{AX}$ *[1 mark]*
   As $AX:XB = 1:3$, AX must be one-quarter of AB, so:
   $\overrightarrow{OX} = \overrightarrow{OA} + \frac{1}{4}\overrightarrow{AB}$
   $\overrightarrow{OX} = 2\mathbf{a} + \frac{1}{4}(\mathbf{b} - 2\mathbf{a})$
   $\overrightarrow{OX} = \frac{3}{2}\mathbf{a} + \frac{1}{4}\mathbf{b}$ *[1 mark]*
   [2 marks available in total — as above]

3 a) $\overrightarrow{BX} = \overrightarrow{BC} + \overrightarrow{CX} = \overrightarrow{BC} - \overrightarrow{XC}$ *[1 mark]*
   $\overrightarrow{BC} = 6\overrightarrow{BW} = 6\mathbf{b}$
   As $AX = 2XC$, CX must be one third of AC, so:
   $\overrightarrow{CX} = -\overrightarrow{XC} = -\frac{1}{3}\overrightarrow{AC}$ (or $\overrightarrow{CX} = \frac{1}{3}\overrightarrow{CA}$) *[1 mark]*
   $\overrightarrow{AC} = \overrightarrow{AB} + \overrightarrow{BC} = 3\mathbf{a} + 6\mathbf{b}$ (or $\overrightarrow{CA} = -3\mathbf{a} - 6\mathbf{b}$)
   $\overrightarrow{CX} = -\frac{1}{3}(3\mathbf{a} + 6\mathbf{b}) = -\mathbf{a} - 2\mathbf{b}$
   $\overrightarrow{BX} = 6\mathbf{b} - \mathbf{a} - 2\mathbf{b} = 4\mathbf{b} - \mathbf{a}$ *[1 mark]*
   [3 marks available in total — as above]
   You could have solved this a little differently, for instance starting by writing $\overrightarrow{BX} = \overrightarrow{BA} + \overrightarrow{AX}$

   b) *From part a) $\overrightarrow{BX} = 4\mathbf{b} - \mathbf{a}$:*
   $ABCD$ is a parallelogram, so:
   $\overrightarrow{CD} = \overrightarrow{BA} = -\overrightarrow{AB} = -3\mathbf{a}$
   $\overrightarrow{CM} = \frac{1}{2}\overrightarrow{CD} = -\frac{3}{2}\mathbf{a}$
   $\overrightarrow{BM} = \overrightarrow{BC} + \overrightarrow{CM}$ *[1 mark]*
   $= 6\mathbf{b} - \frac{3}{2}\mathbf{a} = \frac{3}{2}(4\mathbf{b} - \mathbf{a})$ *[1 mark]*

   B, X and M must be three points on a straight line because the lines BM and BX are both scalar multiples of the vector $4\mathbf{b} - \mathbf{a}$.
   [2 marks available in total — as above]

Section Six — Statistics and Probability

Page 76: Mean, Median, Mode and Range

1 1, 4, 7
   [2 marks available — 2 marks for all three numbers correct, otherwise 1 mark for 3 numbers that have the correct range and mean but aren't all different, or 3 different numbers that have the correct mean or the correct range]

2 Total mark for boys = $15b$
   Total mark for girls = $13g$
   Total number of pupils = $15 + 13 = 28$
   so, mean mark for all pupils = $\dfrac{15b + 13g}{28}$
   [3 marks available — 1 mark for correct total marks for boys and girls, 1 mark for the total number of pupils, 1 mark for correct answer]

3 Total running time for first 20 days = $20 \times 56.2 = 1124$ *[1 mark]*
   Total running time for all 30 days = $30 \times 54.4 = 1632$ *[1 mark]*
   Total running time for last 10 days = $1632 - 1124 = 508$ *[1 mark]*
   Mean running time for last 10 days = $508 \div 10$
                                      = 50.8 minutes *[1 mark]*
   [4 marks available in total — as above]

4 $32 + 23 + 31 + 28 + 36 + 26 = 176$ *[1 mark]*
   $4 \times 27.25 = 109$ *[1 mark]*
   $176 - 109 = 67$ *[1 mark]*
   so, goats weighing 31 kg and 36 kg *[1 mark]*
   [4 marks available in total — as above]

Page 77: Quartiles and Comparing Distributions

1 a) Rewrite data in ascending order:
       3, 4, 4, 5, 5, 6, 7, 7, 8, 8, 9, 10, 11, 11, 12
       The lower quartile is the $(15 + 1) \div 4 = $ 4th value
       So the lower quartile is 5. *[1 mark]*
       The upper quartile is the $3(15 + 1) \div 4 = $ 12th value
       So the upper quartile is 10. *[1 mark]*
       [2 marks available in total — as above]

   b) E.g. The interquartile range will remain the same, as all the values have decreased by 50p. This 50p will cancel out when you subtract the lower quartile from the upper quartile. *[1 mark]*

2 a) Patch A: 8, 8, 9, 12, 13, 14, 14, 16, 18, 19, 22
       lower quartile = 9 (3rd value)
       upper quartile = 18 (9th value)
       IQR = $18 - 9 = 9$

       Patch B: 11, 11, 13, 13, 14, 15, 19
       lower quartile = 11 (2nd value)
       upper quartile = 15 (6th value)
       IQR = $15 - 11 = 4$
       [4 marks available — 2 marks for each correct interquartile range, otherwise 1 mark for each correct lower or upper quartile up to a maximum of 2 marks]

   b) E.g. the interquartile range is smaller in Patch B, so the number of strawberries per plant in Patch B is more consistent. *[1 mark]*

Page 78: Frequency Tables — Finding Averages

1 a) $(0 \times 8) + (1 \times 3) + (2 \times 5) + (3 \times 8) + (4 \times 4) + (5 \times 1) = 58$
       [2 marks available — 1 mark for the correct calculation, 1 mark for the correct answer]

   b) $58 \div 29 = 2$
       [2 marks available — 1 mark for the correct calculation, 1 mark for the correct answer]

2 $(0 \times 2) + (2 \times 4) + (3 \times 7) + (5 \times 11) + (7 \times 6) + (8 \times 3) + (10 \times 3) = 180$
   $180 \div 36 = 5$
   [3 marks available — 1 mark for finding the total number of messages, 1 mark for the correct calculation to find the mean, 1 mark for the correct answer]

Pages 79-80: Grouped Frequency Tables

1 a) There were 32 pupils and $13 + 6 + 1 = 20$ didn't qualify. *[1 mark]*
       $(20 \div 32) \times 100 = 62.5\%$ *[1 mark]*
       [2 marks available in total — as above]

   b) The four quickest runners had times $22 < t \leq 26$.
       Mid-interval value = $(26 + 22) \div 2 = 24$ *[1 mark]*
       $24 \times 4 = 96$ seconds *[1 mark]*
       [2 marks available in total — as above]

2

Hours of exercise	Frequency	Mid-interval value	Frequency × mid-interval value
$0 \leq x < 2$	15	$(0 + 2) \div 2 = 1$	$15 \times 1 = 15$
$2 \leq x < 4$	9	$(2 + 4) \div 2 = 3$	$9 \times 3 = 27$
$4 \leq x < 6$	8	$(4 + 6) \div 2 = 5$	$8 \times 5 = 40$
$6 \leq x < 8$	6	$(6 + 8) \div 2 = 7$	$6 \times 7 = 42$
$8 \leq x < 10$	3	$(8 + 10) \div 2 = 9$	$3 \times 9 = 27$
$10 \leq x < 12$	3	$(10 + 12) \div 2 = 11$	$3 \times 11 = 33$

   $15 + 27 + 40 + 42 + 27 + 33 = 184$ hours
   [3 marks available — 1 mark for all mid-interval values, 1 mark for calculation of frequency × mid-interval value, 1 mark for the correct answer]

3 a) $40 < x \leq 50$ *[1 mark]*

   b)

Exam mark	Frequency	Mid-interval value	Frequency × mid-interval value
$10 < x \leq 20$	2	$(10 + 20) \div 2 = 15$	$2 \times 15 = 30$
$20 < x \leq 30$	5	$(20 + 30) \div 2 = 25$	$5 \times 25 = 125$
$30 < x \leq 40$	7	$(30 + 40) \div 2 = 35$	$7 \times 35 = 245$
$40 < x \leq 50$	8	$(40 + 50) \div 2 = 45$	$8 \times 45 = 360$
$50 < x \leq 60$	4	$(50 + 60) \div 2 = 55$	$4 \times 55 = 220$
$60 < x \leq 70$	6	$(60 + 70) \div 2 = 65$	$6 \times 65 = 390$

   $(30 + 125 + 245 + 360 + 220 + 390) \div 32$
   $= 1370 \div 32 = 42.8125 = 42.8$ (to 3 s.f.)
   [4 marks available — 1 mark for all mid-interval values, 1 mark for calculation of frequency × mid-interval value, 1 mark for dividing 1370 by 32, 1 mark for the correct answer]

4 a) $((1 \times 2) + (4 \times 4) + (7 \times 3) + (10 \times 1)) \div 10 = 49 \div 10 = 4.9$ cm
       [4 marks available — 1 mark for all mid-interval values, 1 mark for calculation of frequency × mid-interval value, 1 mark for dividing 49 by 10, 1 mark for the correct answer]

   b) E.g. As we do not have original data we do not know the exact data values and have to approximate using the mid-interval values. *[1 mark]*

138

Pages 81-82: Cumulative Frequency

1 a)

Exam mark (%)	≤ 20	≤ 30	≤ 40	≤ 50	≤ 60	≤ 70	≤ 80	≤ 100
Cumulative Frequency	3	13	25	49	91	107	116	120

[1 mark]

b)

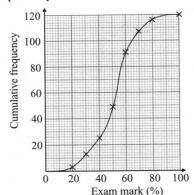

[2 marks available — 1 mark for plotting points correctly,
1 mark for joining them with a smooth curve or straight lines]
A common mistake in exams is not plotting the points at the top
end of the interval. But you wouldn't make that mistake, would you?

c) Median plotted at 60 gives a value of 53%
[1 mark, accept answers ± 2%]

d) Lower quartile at 30 gives a value of 43%
Upper quartile at 90 gives a value of 60%
Inter-quartile range = 60 − 43 = 17%
[2 marks available — 1 mark for correct method,
1 mark for correct answer, accept answers ± 4%]

2 a)

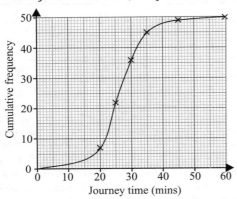

[2 marks available — 1 mark for plotting points correctly,
1 mark for joining them with a smooth curve or straight lines]

b) Number of journeys between 27 and 47 minutes = 49 − 28 = 21
[2 marks available — 1 mark for reading the cumulative
frequencies off at 27 and 47 minutes, 1 mark for correct
answer, accept answers ± 3]

c) 48 journeys took less than 40 mins so 2 journeys took longer.
Percentage of total number = (2 ÷ 50) × 100 = 4%
[2 marks available — 1 mark for correct method,
1 mark for correct answer, accept answers ± 2%]

d) Median of the morning times plotted at 25 gives a 26 minute
journey time. *[1 mark]*
E.g. on average it takes less time to travel in the evening than in
the morning. *[1 mark]*
[2 marks available in total — as above]

Pages 83-84: Histograms and Frequency Density

1

Number of minutes of TV watched (m)	Frequency
$40 \leq m < 60$	20
$60 \leq m < 70$	70
$70 \leq m < 80$	40
$80 \leq m < 120$	80
$120 \leq m < 140$	60

[2 marks available — 1 mark for using
frequency = frequency density × class width,
1 mark for correct answers]

2

[3 marks available — 1 mark for finding frequency densities,
2 marks for all bars drawn correctly, otherwise 1 mark for one bar
drawn correctly]

3 a) Large squares less than 3.5 kg = 4 + 3 = 7
Total number of large squares = 25
(7 ÷ 25) × 100 = 28%
[3 marks available — 1 mark for finding the number of large
squares less than 3.5 kg, 1 mark for the correct calculation,
1 mark for the correct answer]
You could also count the smaller squares to get
(175 ÷ 625) × 100 = 28%.

b) 5 large squares = 45 lambs *[1 mark]*
1 large square = 45 ÷ 5 = 9 lambs
25 large squares = 9 × 25 = 225 lambs *[1 mark]*
[2 marks available in total — as above]

c) From 3.2 kg to 3.5 kg there are 45 small squares and
from 3.5 kg to 6 kg there are 18 big squares. So there are:
45 + (18 × 25) = 495 small squares greater than 3.2 kg *[1 mark]*
From b), 1 large square = 25 small squares = 9 lambs, so
1 small square = 9 ÷ 25 = 0.36 lambs *[1 mark]*
495 small squares = 0.36 × 495 = 178.2 lambs
≈ 178 lambs *[1 mark]*

[3 marks available in total — as above]

Page 85: Probability Basics

1 Probability of not blinking = $1 - \frac{2}{5}$ *[1 mark]*

   $= \frac{3}{5}$ *[1 mark]*

   [2 marks available in total — as above]

2 a) Number of red counters = $10 - 4 = 6$ *[1 mark]*

   Probability of getting a red counter = $\frac{6}{10} = \frac{3}{5}$ *[1 mark]*

   [2 marks available in total — as above]

   b) No green counters so probability of getting a green = 0 *[1 mark]*

3 Let P(spotty sock) = y

   Then P(stripy sock) = $2y$ *[1 mark]*

   $0.4 + y + 2y = 1$ *[1 mark]*

   $3y = 0.6$ *[1 mark]*

   $y = 0.2$

   The probability he gets a spotty sock is 0.2 *[1 mark]*

   [4 marks available in total — as above]

Page 86: Expected Frequency

1 $8 - 3 - 2 = 3$ green sections, so P(green) = $\frac{3}{8}$ or 0.375

   $\frac{3}{8} \times 200 = 75$

   [3 marks available — 1 mark for working out the probability of landing on green, 1 mark for doing probability × no. of trials, 1 mark for the correct answer]

2 P(being born on a Tuesday) = $\frac{1}{7}$ *[1 mark]*

   $\frac{1}{7} \times 834$ *[1 mark]*

   $= 119.1428...$ *[1 mark]*

   ≈ 119 pupils *[1 mark]*

   [4 marks available in total — as above]

3 a) $1 - 0.18 - 0.36 - 0.19 - 0.06 = 0.21$ *[1 mark]*

   b) P(win) = 0.36

   Number of times he wins = 0.36×50 *[1 mark]*

   $= 18$ *[1 mark]*

   Number of times he doesn't win = $50 - 18 = 32$ *[1 mark]*

   [3 marks available in total — as above]

Pages 87-88: The AND / OR Rules

1 a) P(not 2) = 1 − P(2) = 1 − 0.15 = 0.85

   [2 marks available — 1 mark for 1 − 0.15, 1 mark for the correct answer]

   b) P(even) = P(2) + P(4) = 0.15 + 0.25

   $= 0.4$ *[1 mark]*

   So P(odd) = 1 − 0.4 *[1 mark]*

   $= 0.6$ *[1 mark]*

   [3 marks available in total — as above]

   You could answer this by working out P(5) and then adding that to P(1) + P(3) but part c) asks for P(5) which is a bit of a hint that you don't need P(5) to answer b).

   c) *either:* From part b) P(odd) = 0.6

   P(odd) = P(1) + P(3) + P(5)

   $0.6 = 0.3 + 0.2 + P(5)$ *[1 mark]*

   $0.1 = P(5)$ *[1 mark]*

   or: P(5) = 1 − P(1, 2, 3 or 4) *[1 mark]*

   P(5) = 1 − (0.3 + 0.15 + 0.2 + 0.25) = 0.1 *[1 mark]*

   [2 marks available in total — as above]

   d) P(lands on 3 twice) = P(3) × P(3) = 0.2 × 0.2 = 0.04

   [2 marks available — 1 mark for a correct method, 1 mark for the correct final answer]

2 a) P(2 chocolate biscuits) = P(first biscuit is chocolate)

   $\times$ P(second biscuit is chocolate)

   $= \frac{7}{20} \times \frac{6}{19} = \frac{21}{190}$

   [3 marks available — 1 mark for the correct probability for picking each chocolate biscuit, 1 mark for multiplying the probabilities of picking the two chocolate biscuits together, 1 mark for the correct answer]

   b) P(1 chocolate and 1 normal) = P(chocolate then normal)

   + P(normal then chocolate)

   $= \left(\frac{7}{20} \times \frac{13}{19}\right) + \left(\frac{13}{20} \times \frac{7}{19}\right) = 2 \times \frac{13 \times 7}{20 \times 19} = \frac{91}{190}$

   [3 marks available — 1 mark for multiplying the correct probabilities in one case, 1 mark for adding the correct probabilities of both cases together, 1 mark for the correct answer]

3 a) P(fewer than 3 dots) = P(1 dot) + P(2 dots)

   $= \frac{1}{6} + \frac{1}{6} = \frac{2}{6} = \frac{1}{3}$

   [2 marks available — 1 mark finding the probabilities of choosing cards with 1 dot and 2 dots on, 1 mark for the correct answer]

   b) P(sum of dots = 4) = P(1 dot then 3 dots)

   + P(2 dots then 2 dots)

   + P(3 dots then 1 dot)

   $= \left(\frac{1}{6} \times \frac{1}{6}\right) + \left(\frac{1}{6} \times \frac{1}{6}\right) + \left(\frac{1}{6} \times \frac{1}{6}\right) = 3 \times \frac{1}{6 \times 6} = \frac{1}{12}$

   [3 marks available — 1 mark for multiplying the correct probabilities in one case, 1 mark for adding the correct probabilities of all three cases together, 1 mark for the correct answer]

   c) P(sum of dots > 9) ≈ P(4 dots then 6 dots)

   + P(5 dots then 6 dots)

   + P(6 dots then 5 dots)

   $= \left(\frac{1}{6} \times \frac{1}{5}\right) + \left(\frac{1}{6} \times \frac{1}{5}\right) + \left(\frac{1}{6} \times \frac{1}{5}\right)$

   $= 3 \times \frac{1}{6 \times 5} = \frac{1}{10}$

   [3 marks available — 1 mark for multiplying the correct probabilities in one case, 1 mark for adding the correct probabilities of all three cases together, 1 mark for the correct answer]

4 P(2 orange and a brown) = P(orange then orange then brown)

   + P(orange then brown then orange)

   + P(brown then orange then orange)

   $= \left(\frac{12}{20} \times \frac{11}{19} \times \frac{8}{18}\right) + \left(\frac{12}{20} \times \frac{8}{19} \times \frac{11}{18}\right) + \left(\frac{8}{20} \times \frac{12}{19} \times \frac{11}{18}\right)$

   $= 3 \times \frac{12 \times 11 \times 8}{20 \times 19 \times 18} = \frac{44}{95}$

   [3 marks available — 1 mark for multiplying the correct probabilities in one case, 1 mark for adding the correct probabilities of all three cases together, 1 mark for the correct answer]

Pages 89-90: Tree Diagrams

1 a)

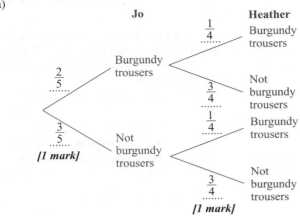

Jo | Heather

[1 mark]

[1 mark]

[2 marks available in total — as above]

b) P(neither wear burgundy trousers) $= \frac{3}{5} \times \frac{3}{4}$ *[1 mark]*

$= \frac{9}{20}$ *[1 mark]*

[2 marks available in total — as above]

2   E.g. use a probability tree diagram:

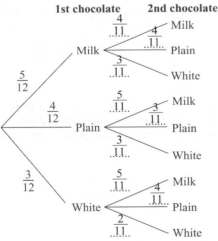

Child 1 | Child 2

[1 mark]

[1 mark]

P(at least one of them has the disease)
= 1 − P(neither have the disease) *[1 mark]*
= 1 − (0.75 × 0.75) *[1 mark]*
= 1 − 0.5625 = 0.4375 *[1 mark]*

[5 marks available in total — as above]

3   a)

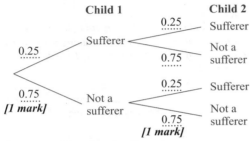

1st chocolate | 2nd chocolate

*[2 marks available — 2 marks for all probabilities correct,
1 mark for four or more probabilities correct]*

b) Outcomes that are one milk and one white: MW and WM
P(one milk and one white) = P(MW) + P(WM)

$= \left(\frac{5}{12} \times \frac{3}{11}\right) + \left(\frac{3}{12} \times \frac{5}{11}\right) = \frac{5}{22}$

*[3 marks available — 1 mark for multiplying the probabilities
of the two chocolates together, 1 mark for adding the
probabilities for each possible case together,
1 mark for the correct answer]*

c) P(at least 1 plain) = 1 − P(no plain)
= 1 − (P(MM) + P(WW) + P(one milk and one white))

$= 1 - \left(\left(\frac{5}{12} \times \frac{4}{11}\right) + \left(\frac{3}{12} \times \frac{2}{11}\right) + \frac{5}{22}\right)$

$= 1 - \left(\frac{10}{66} + \frac{3}{66} + \frac{15}{66}\right) = 1 - \frac{28}{66} = \frac{38}{66} = \frac{19}{33}$

*[3 marks available — 1 mark for working out at least one of
P(MM) and P(WW) correctly, 1 mark for a correct
calculation to find the answer, 1 mark for the correct answer]*
You could also answer this by working out P(first one plain) +
P(MP) + P(WP), but it's a bit more work to get to the answer.

How to get answers for the Practice Papers

You can print out worked solutions to Practice Papers
1 & 2 by accessing your free Online Edition of this book.

There's more info about how to get your Online Edition
at the front of this book.